The Legend of Proposition 13

The Legend of Proposition 13

The Great California Tax Revolt

JOEL FOX

To order additional copies of this book, contact:
Xlibris Corporation
1-888-795-4274
www.Xlibris.com
Orders@Xlibris.com
17928-FOX1

To the thousands of California taxpayers who created the legend and to those that maintain it

And

To the memory of Larry Straw, attorney and friend of the Howard Jarvis Taxpayers Association

CONTENTS

Acknowledgement

While I participated in a number of the events reported in this book, and was familiar with many others, the memory does get rusty. I appreciate the people who helped me remember through conversations or writings.

I would like to thank Estelle Jarvis, Dolores Tuttle, and the other members of the Board of Directors and the staff of the Howard Jarvis Taxpayers Association, for their time and access to records and papers. Especially, I'd like to thank Executive Director Kris Vosburgh and Administrative Assistant Ed Thomas who knew how to keep files better than I ever did and knew where to find them.

I would like to express my thanks to Nancy Reagan, Joanne Drake, chief of staff in the Office of President Ronald Reagan, and Greg Cumming and the staff at the Ronald Reagan Presidential Library for granting me access to papers, particularly the radio commentaries, and for their general help and assistance at the Library.

Thank you also to Gary Kurutz, principal librarian, Special Collections Branch, and staff at the California State Library for their cooperation in accessing the Howard Jarvis and Proposition 13 files.

To those who spent some time with me reminiscing about the last 25 years of California and national politics, I appreciate your indulgence. To Martin Anderson, Chuck Betz, Jerry Brown, Bill Butcher, Jack Cohen, Jon Coupal, Dave Doerr, Harvey Englander, Lenny Goldberg, Trevor Grimm, Allan Hoffenblum, Ross Johnson, Jim Lacy, Stu Mollrich, George Putnam and Kris Vosburgh, thank you.

Invaluable was my copy of *I'm Mad as Hell* by Howard Jarvis and Robert Pack. For anyone who wants to know anything about California taxation, there is one great source, Dave Doerr's book, *California's Tax Machine*. I also found the following works important and helpful on the subject of Proposition 13: *Secrets of the Tax Revolt* by James Ring Adams; *The Tax Revolt* by Alvin Rabushka and Pauline Ryan; and *Paradise Lost* by Peter Schrag.

Thank you to Trevor Grimm who edited the book.

Any errors in the telling of the following story are mine alone.

Joel Fox
Los Angeles
January 2003

Introduction

Jon Coupal, President
Howard Jarvis Taxpayers Association

Ours is a nation founded on a tax revolt. The Founders recognized that citizens would never enjoy liberty as long as they were taxed without representation. Once having secured independence, they framed our Constitution with ten initial amendments, called the Bill of Rights, that were intended to protect citizens from potential abuses of the people by their government.

Our California experience prior to the passage of Proposition 13 taught us that even with representation, our freedoms could be threatened. The lesson especially is true when members of the Legislature are corrupt, or indolent or incompetent or all three. When peoples' homes literally were being taken through the power of the tax collector, we knew that we had lost our way and had deviated from the ideal of a government "of the people, by the people, and for the people."

With the passage of Proposition 13, Howard Jarvis, Paul Gann and their millions of supporters made a resounding statement – without the use of cannon fire – that it is the people who will rule. Called by many "the tax revolt", Proposition 13 was, in fact, an evolutionary expansion of the citizens' rights guaranteed in the United States Constitution. As with the American Revolution, Proposition 13 acknowledges that one of government's most abused powers is the ability to take the livelihood and property of the people through taxation. By limiting taxes and by giving the people a say in how much they would pay to support government, Californians sent a message thundering across the nation—one that is still reverberating!

In California, polls repeatedly have shown that if they had it to do over, voters again would overwhelmingly approve Proposition 13. But the changes that Proposition 13 brought to California government – limiting taxes and providing the right to vote on taxes – have not taken place without opposition.

Since its inception, Proposition 13 has had powerful enemies. Politicians have opposed it because they see it as limiting their power. Public employee unions have resisted it because they see any restriction on government's ability to tax as a threat to their jobs and wages. Some in the business community continue to fight it because they either want to curry the favor of government or want to avoid paying their fair share of taxes. And, of course, many pundits still doubt the peoples' ability to make important decisions about how they should be governed.

Today, with the state of California facing the largest budget shortfall of any state in history, the fate of Proposition 13 is still in question. In spite of the fact that our budget problems have been brought about by lavish overspending, the politicians consider Proposition 13 fair game.

The *Legend of Proposition 13*, written by my long-time friend and colleague, Joel Fox, tells a story that is as important today as it was 25 years ago when the voters made Proposition 13 law. First as a senior aide to Howard Jarvis, and then, after Howard's passing, as president of the Howard Jarvis Taxpayers Association for 12 years, Joel was at ground zero for many of the most critical events that surrounded Proposition 13. Since stepping down as president of the taxpayer organization in 1998, Joel has continued to provide good counsel and active support for the taxpayers' cause.

While the book deals with vital taxpayer issues, much of it is devoted to the fascinating and often entertaining stories of the players, both major and minor, that made Proposition 13 a reality, and stories of those who have labored, often against long odds, to keep Proposition 13 in force and its spirit alive for a quarter-century.

The Howard Jarvis Taxpayers Association is dedicated to protecting and advancing taxpayers' rights. Central to these rights in California is Proposition 13. I hope that you will enjoy this book, that it brings greater understanding of what has become, like the Boston Tea Party, an icon of taxpayer freedom, and that you will be inspired by what thousands of ordinary citizens working together can accomplish to make possible a system of fair and reasonable taxation. The fight goes on!

Author's Note

If you find the term "fiscalization of land use" beyond this page, you have my permission to rip up this book. "Fiscalization of land use" is bureaucratic-speak for a type of taxing policy, which emerged in California since the Proposition 13 tax revolt. This book is not about detailed tax policy and puzzling terminology, although you will read some plain tax arguments here and there. Nor is this book an academic treatise. However, there are some numbers in the book—they could not be avoided.

Many books and papers have been written about Proposition 13 and tax policy, or Proposition 13 and governance. However, what is misunderstood about the Proposition 13 tax revolt is that it was not only about numbers and politics and the governing process but, more importantly, it was about emotion and spirit and freedom. In this regard, the Proposition 13 story is the stuff of legends. It is about folk heroes who stood up for the freedom to take control of their lives.

I watched the Proposition 13 story unfold first hand. I followed the Proposition 13 campaign closely and soon after the initiative passed, joined Howard Jarvis as an aide, quickly becoming executive director of his taxpayers' association and finally serving as president of the association for 12 years.

This is the story of the hard work, odd tales, and bizarre arguments that popped up on the tax revolt trail. This also is the story of a modern-day folk hero, Howard Jarvis, and a legend in the making, Proposition 13.

PART ONE

Legends and Folk Heroes

Mystery and Mystique

A middle-aged woman traveled the 30 miles from her home in the San Fernando Valley to the Los Angeles County Hall of Administration to plead her case directly with county officials. It was the mid-1960s and the woman had received her property tax bill from the county with a tax she could not possibly afford. Like many California residents at that time, she had shuddered with fear when opening her property tax bill. The taxes had been escalating at an outrageous pace in recent years and many people could not make the payments required of them. The woman reasoned that if she could make her case directly to county officials, they surely would reduce her taxes.

Accompanying her on the trip to downtown Los Angeles was Howard Jarvis, a retired businessman who had been on a crusade to reduce property taxes for five years.

The woman argued her case in vain. County officials told her that her taxes had been calculated properly and according to law and that the amount on the bill was what she had to pay. The shock and frustration proved too great for her. The woman had a heart attack in the county building and died.

Jarvis was outraged. No one should die because of prohibitive property taxes. He became defiant. He swore to change the property tax system in California. And, he created a slogan out of this tragedy to lead his effort: "While death and taxes may be inevitable, being taxed to death is not inevitable."

A decade later, he would lead the greatest tax revolt since the legendary Boston Tea Party, the campaign to pass Proposition 13, and he helped create a legend of his own.

Not too long ago, at a Mystery Writers Conference in Albuquerque, New Mexico, a dozen writers were sitting around a lunch table talking about politics. No one remembered how the conversation had veered in that direction, but the suspicion was that one of the authors was considering using a politician as a villain in a story. The writers did not speak highly of politicians that day. In fact, the actions of the political class were being derided in the way Americans have derided them for centuries.

One writer, now of New Mexico, but formerly of California, concluded the conversation by saying, "There was only one law that ever really helped the ordinary guy. That Jarvis Proposition 13 when I lived in California."

It is not surprising, twenty-five years after Proposition 13 was passed, to hear that sentiment expressed. Even now, people remember how rising tax bills in California were threatening their home ownership. Children remember how their parents feared that they could not meet their property tax obligations and still have enough money to provide the necessities of life for their families. And they remember how Howard Jarvis led a tax revolt that kept alive their piece of the American Dream.

Republican California State Senator Tom McClintock said he still has a vivid memory of the "relief in my parents' eyes when Proposition 13 passed. There were serious discussions around the dinner table if we were going to hang on to the house given the huge escalation in property taxes. To my parents, Howard Jarvis was a saint."

And, former Democratic State Senator and now chairman of the California Democratic Party, Art Torres, told a gathering in 1991 that he realized that he was wrong about opposing Proposition 13. He since had seen how it helped seniors in his neighborhood, and even young families starting out, to get a home.

Recently, at a television show I appeared on, the producer insisted on walking me out to the parking lot to take the opportunity to thank me, as a representative of the Howard Jarvis Taxpayers Association, for saving her home. That act of "saving" her home was almost twenty-five years ago but it was something she could not forget.

However, not everyone sees Proposition 13 in the same light.

When the interstate highway collapsed during the 1989 Loma Prieta earthquake in the San Francisco Bay Area, an editorial cartoon in the *Los Angeles Times* showed a car crushed by a freeway, and the license plate of the car read: Prop 13.

When 12-year-old Polly Klass was abducted from her home in Petaluma, California, north of San Francisco, and brutally murdered, Proposition 13 was judged as culpable by national columnist and noted author Richard Reeves in a *Money* magazine article. Reeves wrote that the killer might have been apprehended before the murder took place if only the police had the advanced communication equipment surely denied them by the Proposition 13 tax cuts.

How absurd can the claims get? Try this one. In his TRB column in the *New Republic* of October 23, 1995, Robert Wright listed his reasons why the O. J. Simpson criminal trial ended without a conviction. His number one reason—Howard Jarvis and Proposition 13!

Wright argued that because Proposition 13 cut taxes, the city and county of Los Angeles had inadequate funds to hire a competent coroner and competent police officials—and, basically, you get what you pay for. The problem with his theory is that it's wrong. At that time, on every rung of the ladder from rookie cop on up, the Los Angeles Police

Department paid higher salaries than the police departments in the other two largest cities in the country—New York and Chicago.

In biblical times, unexpected terrors called "plagues" were thought to come from the hand of God. In twentieth—and twenty-first-century California, modern "plagues" apparently are the result of Proposition 13.

For many politicians, bureaucrats and members of the media who don't trust the people taking political power into their own hands, Proposition 13 has been and continues to be the scapegoat for all the ills that befall California.

It is not surprising that Proposition 13 is blamed for all of California's problems. The bureaucracy does not miss an opportunity to blame Prop 13 for its own failings or faulty service as they repeat the mantra: "It's Proposition 13's fault."

Unfortunately, children have been murdered, bridges have collapsed, and public services have stalled in other states over the same time period, but these states did not have a tax cut initiative like Proposition 13. New York librarians began a misery index to record library closures. Could Proposition 13 have caused this problem all the way across the country? Frankly, it's no surprise if someone said, "Yes, it was the Proposition 13 mentality that caused the problem."

Proposition 13 has been successful at what it promised to do. It prevented people from being taxed out of their homes and, for the first time, it gave property owners a measure of certainty over their taxes.

In the early 1800s, U.S. Supreme Court Chief Justice John Marshall wrote that the only protection the people had against unwise and excessive taxation was the wisdom and justice of the legislative body. That protection proved as worthless as your typical political campaign promise.

In California, voters found they had to protect

themselves from unwise and excessive taxation and they had the means to do it with the initiative process.

The initiative process allows people to write their own laws. After enough signatures are gathered to qualify a measure for the ballot, it is given a number. The property tax measure submitted by Howard Jarvis for the June 1978 California primary election ballot got the number that would later add to its mystique: 13.

And, 25 years after it became law, the discussion of its merits still is hot.

What Proposition 13 Did

Proposition 13, passed overwhelmingly by California voters on June 6, 1978, was the greatest tax revolt in this country's history since the Boston Tea Party. But, before getting into the story of how it came about, here is a word about what it actually did.

Proposition 13 changed the tax laws of California. It reduced property taxes on homes, businesses, farms and other property by about 57 % or a total of about $7 billion. Under Proposition 13, now a part of the state constitution, property tax rates could not exceed 1% of the property's market value and, absent a sale or major remodeling, market value increases were capped at a maximum of 2% per year.

Prior to Proposition 13, the tax rate throughout California averaged a little less than 3% of market value, and there were no limits on increases either for the tax rate or the market value placed on property. Some properties were reassessed upwards by 50% to 100% in just one year and their owners' tax bills, as a percentage of that increased value, jumped correspondingly. Under the tax cut measure, property valuations were rolled back to their 1975–76 levels. If a property were sold, the property could be reassessed at 1% of the new market value with the 2% cap placed on any annual increase. Thus, a new buyer would know both what the taxes would be and what the maximum amount of property tax increase annually he or she could expect for as long as he or she owned the property.

In addition to capping property taxes, Proposition 13 required that all state tax rate increases be approved by a two-thirds vote of the legislature and that local special tax increases had to be approved by a two-thirds vote of the people. The people's right to vote on taxes is a key taxpayer protection but one not often exercised until Proposition 13 came along.

If one wants to figure out what the property taxes now would be under the pre-Proposition 13 system, just multiply the property's current value by 3%. Most people are shocked after they perform the calculation.

Simply put, Proposition 13 cut property taxes and put in place a new property tax system. That's what Proposition 13 did, but that's not all that it was about. The story of Proposition 13 is about people rising up behind a colorful, determined leader to free themselves from a taxpayers' nightmare.

The Romance of Taxes

Romantic tales we have all grown up with, which tell about a quest for freedom, often cite taxes as the weapon of oppression. A hero takes decisive action to free the oppressed people and overthrow the tax collector. These adventures could be called "The Romance of Taxes." The similarities with the Proposition 13 victory are readily apparent.

The joining of *romance* and *taxes* would seem possible only by a shotgun ceremony. Death and Taxes is more like it – somber terms, befitting the subjects. But, there is a Romance to Taxes, for the dry subject of taxes is an important ingredient in some of our favorite stories, re-told from generation to generation. Think of Robin Hood, Lady Godiva, William Tell, Zorro, and most assuredly, the Patriots of the Boston Tea Party, among the tax-resisting heroes.

Contemporary audiences still respond to these stories. We all learned well the lessons from those stories we heard, read, or watched as children.

And for those who are tired of hearing that opposition to taxes makes you an enemy of civilization, take note that you stand at the side of mythical and revered heroes.

Look at the themes running through the California Tax Revolt.

Proposition 13 was an uprising of the people against an uncaring government which would just as soon see the people lose their homes for non-payment of taxes than worry if they would have to live homeless, say, in a forest, which is similar to the story of Robin Hood legend.

Some say Robin Hood took from the rich and gave to the poor. Look closer at the legend. The people were made poor by the actions of the authorities – the government. The chief villains of the tale are Prince John, the head of the national government, and the sheriff of Nottingham, in charge of the local government and the chief tax collector.

The rich that Robin took from became rich because they levied taxes. The poor he gave to were poor because they paid the extraordinary taxes. Robin was a hero because he returned this money to its rightful owners.

The artists who created the memorable film, *The Adventures of Robin Hood,* starring Errol Flynn, saw the story the same way. The entire movie is set up the first time Prince John appears on screen, when he says to an ally: "Golden days are ahead. I will assign tax districts to you tomorrow."

In the Great Hall of Nottingham Castle, where Robin Hood first meets Prince John, he says: "We Saxons have little to fatten on by the time your tax gathers are through."

The Adventures of Robin Hood is a film about heroes reclaiming freedom that was first crushed by the weight of heavy taxes.

Since Proposition 13 was a California tax revolt, it is appropriate to include the fictional story of Zorro who defended the people from the corrupt *alcalde*, or mayor, in early Los Angeles.

Here, too, movies enhance the legend we all know. In the 1940 Tyrone Power film, *The Mark of Zorro*, when Don Diego Vega (later Zorro) arrives home to California from Spain, he learns from a San Pedro tavern owner why his carriage driver is mute. "At a meeting of the peons, this man spoke against the heavy taxes. The next day, the soldiers of His Excellency cut out his tongue."

These heroes want to free people from unjust taxes that are crushing them and in order to do so, they are forced to fight the entrenched authority, just as Howard Jarvis did with Proposition 13. He said, "My taxes don't worry me. I'm worried about the guy who can't pay his taxes."

The idea that taxes can eliminate freedom was told nicely in a passage in Mark Twain's *Connecticut Yankee in King Arthur's Court*. Twain crafted a timeless legend to hoist the banner of education over ignorance and freedom over slavery. He derided the term "freeman" in King Arthur's England – the passage described Twain's time and our time as well. The Yankee said, once the harvest was in: "Then came the procession of robbers to levy their blackmail upon it ... there were taxes, and taxes, and taxes, and more taxes, and taxes again, and yet other taxes—upon this free and independent pauper ...."

The rally against taxes is a fight to secure freedom. Freedom is the value at the core of these re-told stories, and taxes are the shackles that hold down that freedom. When taxation is too heavy, people revolt. The Proposition 13 tax revolt is the stuff of legends, on par with any of the re-told stories and folk tales.

Proposition 13, too, is about freedom. In fact, freedom was a constant goal of Howard Jarvis. In his syndicated radio commentary *Byline*, which was broadcast for a few years after Proposition 13 passed, Jarvis said, "I have fought for freedom, spoken for freedom, and written about freedom all my life. I cannot stop doing those things because I know once you stop working for freedom, you lose it. It can be taken away with military force as in Poland, or it can be chipped away by people in positions of power who claim they are taking something from you to give to the common good."

Jarvis revisited this theme in another *Byline* commentary.

"Someone once said taxes are what we pay for a civilized society. Fair enough. But, let me add a Jarvis corollary: Tax cuts produce a freer society. In our free society, we believe that a man belongs only to himself, that he earns the rewards of his labors. If a government, through taxation, took it all away, the individual would be a slave to that government. As of now, about half of what we earn goes to federal, state, and local governments in taxes. We are only half free. Tax cuts will give us more freedom."

U.S. Supreme Court Justice Oliver Wendell Holmes was the person who said that taxes are what we pay for a civilized society. It should be noted that Holmes made his famous remark in 1904, almost a decade before the income tax was sanctioned. Taxes in 1904 took seven percent of average incomes.

Sometimes, to stop taxes from destroying the people, they have to rise up behind a champion and fight back. That's how legends are born. In that sense, the story of Proposition 13 is no different from other familiar and cherished legends.

Folklore

Folklore is the people's story. The elites or the universities or the newspaper writers do not hand it down; it's passed along by the people. For Proposition 13 and Howard Jarvis, that is a good thing. The people have a different view on what happened with Proposition 13 which is often ignored by professors and newspaper writers.

Long-time editorial page editor for the *Sacramento Bee*, Peter Schrag, argued that Proposition 13's tax limitations led to the "Mississippification" of many California public institutions, especially the schools. This was a term he coined by which he meant that the services were as run down as those in the low-tax, perennially lowly ranked state of Mississippi.

However, to Mr. and Mrs. A. G. Isgreen of Hermosa Beach, Proposition 13 meant something else. They saw the taxes on their house and two small rental properties increase by 140% in one year. They wrote to the *Hermosa Beach Easy Reader* about one week before the vote on Proposition 13: "We have lived here for 36 years and just retired. Proposition 13 must be passed or we will be wiped out. It's no joke!"

Proposition 13 was not about tax cuts for the rich – the rich always have enough money to pay their taxes – it was about helping the average working or retired person keep the home that they had managed to purchase by scraping enough money together. In many respects, critics of Proposition 13 who wail that cutting off tax dollars hurts the little guy don't understand that Proposition 13 itself helped the little guy. Proposition 13 was, in reality, a social movement that allowed housing to remain affordable. Affordable housing is a big problem. Proposition 13 stopped the government from adding to that problem by forcing people away from their homes with inflated property taxes.

No matter what the editorial pages of the *Los Angeles Times* or *Sacramento Bee* or *San Francisco Chronicle* say, the people respect Proposition 13. Like any good folklore, the story of Proposition 13 will be re-told as a time when the people rose up against great odds, and won.

As early as 1982, Milt Policzer wrote in the *Los Angeles Daily Journal*, a newspaper that expressly covers the legal community, that like a star athlete's uniform number, Proposition 13 should be retired from re-use on statewide ballots. Numbers recycle on the propositions after a set number of years. Policzer argued that no other proposition so readily conjures up an image of what it's about than Proposition 13; that Prop 13's fame is nationwide; and that it would be unfair to confuse voters, writers and lawyers with a new Proposition 13.

In 1999, State Senator Ross Johnson, one of the so-called Proposition 13 Babies because he was first elected to the legislature as a strong supporter of Proposition 13, introduced a bill to retire the number Proposition 13. Like Policzer, Johnson argued that using Proposition 13 to label a new ballot measure would only confuse people who had become comfortable with the famous tax-cutting Proposition 13 of 1978.

The analysis of Johnson's bill, written by senate staffers, sniffed, Wouldn't retiring the number 13 be "viewed by most observers as a means to honor Proposition 13 ...?"

Exactly. Was retiring the number supposed to be a bad thing? Perhaps it upset the sensibilities of government officials who didn't like the power Proposition 13 held over them.

To prevent the number 13 being used in the upcoming 2000 election, when a new Proposition 13 was to be designated, Johnson's bill had to receive a two-thirds vote as an urgency measure. It received a majority vote but not the two-thirds required, and so it failed.

Just as well. Proposition 13 does not need special treatment from government to achieve legitimacy. It already has been elevated to special status by California taxpayers who, after two and a half decades, still support it overwhelmingly in poll after poll.

Folk Hero

By leading the tax revolt to make things better for people and standing up to the threats, the belittling and the abuse that comes with challenging the status quo, Howard Jarvis became a folk hero.

Jarvis was given folk hero status almost immediately after Prop 13 passed. Ed Busch, a talk show host on WFAA Radio, wrote in the supplement to the *Dallas Morning News* in December 1978: "In future American history books, Howard Jarvis will probably be remembered as a very real folk hero in a day when such heroes did not exist. He is a character in a true, and sometimes forgotten, sense of the word."

Five years later, that opinion was affirmed in the pages of the *Arizona Morning News*: "For Howard Jarvis, like him or not, is a folk hero and we don't have many of those around anymore. A folk hero can come from any walk of life, but the beginnings are usually humble . . . matched with incredible intelligence can produce an unforgettable individual whose wit and wisdom last long after the person has passed on. Howard Jarvis . . . (is) about the best we have who's living today."

Jarvis was often characterized as a curmudgeon, a character, colorful. His political enemies used much worse descriptions. Jarvis had a bulldog approach in debates and often characterized opponents as "popcorn balls," and the like.

Former California governor and current Oakland mayor Jerry Brown, remembers Jarvis as, "Exuberant and self-motivated. He had to be self-motivated because everyone was against him."

National political columnist Mary McGrory, the day after Prop 13 passed, labeled Jarvis "a 75-year-old barking dog Republican conservative." Jarvis took the name-calling in stride, but admitted, "You need iron pants to be in this business."

In an interview by A. F. Decker in the *AirCal Magazine*, July 1984, Jarvis agreed he was colorful, and when asked if that was part of his success, he replied, "Oh, I don't think there's any question about it."

Bill Monroe, host of *Meet the Press*, nearly two weeks after Proposition 13 passed, noted to Jarvis that, "in all those years of anti-tax crusading, people were calling you a crank, a curmudgeon, a kook and you were getting nowhere. This year, all of a sudden, you have got a two-to-one victory."

Jarvis replied: "You know, they called Edison a nut because he said he was going to produce some light out of a silk thread in a bottle, and when somebody pushed the button and the lights came on, he wasn't a nut anymore."

Political ally Ross Johnson said the public image of Jarvis was that of an irascible guy, but that the image grew out of Jarvis's political skills. "He was very good; he had real skill at sticking to his message. That's why people thought he was irascible because he wouldn't answer their questions. He would say, 'That's not the question' . . . or 'My question has priority over yours.' Howard Jarvis was a natural at staying on message, a style not obvious to people. They took it for irascibility."

Whatever it was, it worked. And, Jarvis's style especially

struck home with hardworking taxpayers who saw taxes mount with no corresponding improvements in government services.

Time Magazine, in recognizing Jarvis as one of the four runners-up for the 1978 Man of the Year Award, said Jarvis was transformed "into a national symbol of middle-class Americans' mounting anger with expensive government programs that yield too few benefits, big budget deficits, and intrusive government regulations."

When the taxes continued to go up, the taxpayers approved of their champion verbally striking back at seemingly uncaring public officials. He trumped the old saying that "You can't fight City Hall." Jarvis became the symbol of someone who not only fought City Hall but won, big-time. The world recognized the victory. Jarvis once received a call from the promoters of an about-to-be-released movie called *Turk 182* starring Timothy Hutton. It was the story of a young man who protested his brother's treatment at the hands of city bureaucrats and mounted an activist campaign to make things right. The promoters wanted to use Jarvis's reputation of the "Man who beat City Hall" to promote the movie.

Nothing came of this effort, but Jarvis's stature as a folk hero got him an acting role in the hilarious spoof of airline disaster movies, *Airplane.* Jarvis played a man who hailed a taxi at the beginning of the movie at LAX, got in and watched the driver, played by Robert Hays, run into the terminal saying he'd be right back. Hays boarded an airplane in pursuit of his true love who was about to leave him. Jarvis waited and waited and waited for the driver to return to the cab with one eye on the running meter! He waited right through the end of the movie's final credits and then appeared on screen one last time sitting in the back of the cab, looked at his watch, and declared, "I'll give him ten more minutes, but that's it."

The joke was Jarvis would never have stood for paying

the charge run up on the cab meter, and everyone knew it.

Jarvis wasn't enamored with the job of being an actor. When *Airplane* producer Howard Koch asked him to do the role, Jarvis replied, "I'm no actor. He (Koch) says, 'Well you don't have to know anything to be an actor' which I guess is true. So I agreed ... It took them eight hours to film my two or three minutes."

Not that he thought he had movie star looks. The heavy-jowled Jarvis was described in a national magazine as having a face which is like a mudslide. That tickled Jarvis, and he often repeated it – to the consternation of his wife, Estelle.

Well, as someone once said, politics is show business for ugly people.

"It stood me in good stead for Proposition 13"

Of course, Howard Jarvis was not a folk hero before Proposition 13 made history. He was a man with a cause—cutting taxes. He had a simple rule of economics when it came to government. "You can't take out more water from a bucket than you put in," he used to say. With deficit spending, government tried, and when officials realized they were short, they just hit up the taxpayers for more money.

Jarvis didn't think this was the way government should work. He ran for mayor of Los Angeles in 1976 just so he'd have a platform to speak out on lowering property taxes. Jarvis told his attorney, Trevor Grimm, later general counsel for the Howard Jarvis Taxpayers Association, "The first thing I'm going to do if I win this election is put a big sign on the door of the mayor's office, and do you know what it's going to say?"

"No," said Grimm.

"That's exactly right," Jarvis said, "NO!"

Jarvis wasn't against government. In 1980, Jarvis told a reporter from Utah's *Magna Times*, a newspaper he once owned in the 1920s and '30s, that, "One of the first things I did as editor was run a campaign for the gym at Cyprus High School." He just was against government run poorly and at too great a cost.

At an early age, Jarvis also was concerned with unfair taxation. He served on the Utah State Tax Commission and got involved in many issues to lower taxes and make government more efficient. He got the appointment because Governor George Dern had read many of the tax editorials Jarvis wrote for his newspapers.

Jarvis grew up in Magna, about 18 miles west of Salt Lake City. He received a law degree from the University of Utah but instead of going into law practice, he decided to buy his hometown weekly newspaper. Gaining national advertising business for his weekly at a time when it was uncommon for weeklies to land national sponsors, Jarvis prospered, building a chain of weekly papers. Soon, he became involved in the Utah State Press Association and, at 24 years of age, became its youngest member in 1927. Eventually, he became president of the association and made a triumphant return as the keynote speaker at the association's annual meeting a couple of years after the passage of Proposition 13 made him a national figure.

While the newspaper business produced a good living, politics had Jarvis's heart. First, he became involved in Republican politics in Utah. Eventually, that involvement led him to the Republican National Executive Committee meeting in Chicago in 1934. Jarvis had taken a hotel room with two beds. He got a call from the hotel manager. The hotel was short of beds and needed to take care of a

California delegate to the meeting. Would Jarvis mind sharing a room?

Jarvis said: "Send him up," and soon he was saying hello to his fellow delegate, Alameda County district attorney, Earl Warren. According to Jarvis, it was Warren, who later would serve as Governor of California and Chief Justice of the United States Supreme Court, who convinced him to seek new opportunities in California.

Jarvis sold his newspapers, moved to southern California, and began a successful manufacturing business.

But he always stayed interested in politics and in taxation. Jarvis worked on the presidential campaigns of both Dwight Eisenhower and Richard Nixon. Then he decided to run for office himself. In 1962, Jarvis challenged incumbent Republican U.S. Senator Thomas Kutchel, complaining that Kutchel too often voted with the Democrats. Converting an old bread truck to a campaign vehicle with a sound system on top, he took his case to the people in all 58 California counties. He finished third in the primary.

Jarvis attempted another run for elective office in 1970, seeking a seat on the State Board of Equalization, which oversees tax policy in the state. This position would have been much like the appointed job he had on the Utah State Tax Commission over 35 years before. However, Jarvis did not spend too much time talking about his candidacy. In campaign stops, he focused his speech on two things: controlling the property tax and re-electing Ronald Reagan as governor.

At an appearance in Santa Barbara, Jarvis talked about his two favorite subjects. When he finished, someone in the audience asked him why he hadn't mentioned he was on the ballot. Jarvis responded that he was interested first in taxes, second in Reagan, and if anyone wanted to vote for him, that was okay, too. His answer got a loud applause. After that, in hopes of eliciting the same audience response,

Jarvis planted someone at all his appearances and, according to plan, the man asked the same question that Jarvis got in Santa Barbara. Jarvis thought the question and his response would help him win over the audience; however, he lost the election.

It was the rapidly rising property taxes that took up Jarvis's full attention. "To have a government levy an absolutely confiscatory tax on a house and for them to foreclose people's homes for taxes, I think, is a high crime and misdemeanor on the part of government; I'd like to impeach them all for it."

Jarvis set out to do something about this "high crime."

His years of political experience made him ready for the tough opposition he would face, as he explained with an unusual story.

Because of his newspaper experience and connection with the Republican National Committee, Jarvis was asked to serve as a press person on a train trip with President Herbert Hoover during his uphill campaign for re-election against Franklin D. Roosevelt. Beyond the normal duties of a press person, the young Jarvis also took on the job of protecting the president from upset citizens suffering from the effects of the Depression. Jarvis described his responsibility as that of standing next to the president at the rear of the train as the president spoke. "I was up there with a pillow so I could knock down anything they threw at him. I was an advance man in the true sense of the word. I'll bet I saved him from getting hit with 500 tomatoes. It stood me in good stead for Proposition 13."

Jarvis told a lot of good stories about being involved in high-profile events. He was on the campaign trail with Hoover; he was in the room when Franklin Roosevelt gave his first speech on social security; he hung around with Clark Gable and Gary Cooper in Hollywood; he wrote a privately published book for J. Paul Getty on his family's involvement in the oil business while working in the cellar of the Getty mansion.

Yes, one had to wonder about all these stories. Were any of these tall tales? One day, I was in the office by myself when there was a knock on the door. A man came in and identified himself as a reporter for the *Boston Globe*. He was writing a book on J. Paul Getty and in the company's private library, he had discovered a fancy-bound, privately published book on the Getty family and its oil business, written by Howard Jarvis. He wanted to set up an appointment to interview Howard about his experience working on the book with Getty.

You never knew.

PART TWO

Before Proposition 13

Ordinary People

As Howard Jarvis remembered it, the beginning of the fight for property tax reform—what became Proposition 13—began in a home on Los Feliz Boulevard in Los Angeles in 1962. He said about twenty people attended the first meeting, "ordinary people," no "big wheels" among them. They had gathered because of their concern about the rising property tax, which was beginning to force elderly people on fixed incomes to give up their homes. As the situation got worse over the years, Jarvis would refer to the circumstance of government taking over homes for non-payment of taxes as "grand felony theft."

While Proposition 13 would become a symbol of tax reduction and the people taking back their government, its most immediate effect was to save people's homes. Taxpayers should not unfairly lose their homes to the whims of inflation and arbitrary tax rate decisions made by spendthrift politicians.

As Jarvis noted, "Proposition 13 was needed mostly because property taxes are the only form of taxes that have no relation to the ability of someone to pay them."

Homes did not produce income, yet either a tax rate increase or a property value assessment increase easily could outstrip any increase in a person's income or ability to pay, especially if the homeowner lived on a fixed income. Some have argued that it is fair to tax the increased value of the home because as a homeowner, one's wealth (not income) increased with the increase in home value. It is a specious argument because the tax collector wants hard currency, coin of the realm, and you can't pay taxes with paper profits based on the increased value of real property.

The twenty people who met in Los Angeles in 1962 understood this truth. They were ordinary people who fit the mold of those who would create Prop 13's folklore. Others soon joined them. Like Jarvis, they all were committed to a long-term battle. Many belonged to different taxpayer groups, but they came together under the banner of Jarvis's United Organizations of Taxpayers. They included Mike Rubino, who had started a homeowners' group in the San Gabriel Valley, and Jimmy Christo, who served as vice-chairman under Chairman Jarvis at the United Organizations of Taxpayers. At the tenth anniversary party for Proposition 13, Christo gave a moving speech about all the hard work and failures that had gone into the tax limitation effort before the Prop 13 success. Christo's dedication to the tax revolt was life-long. Until his death at the age of 96 in January 2003, he drove his car with personalized license plates that read: Yes on 13.

Harley Cole, who would later serve on the board of the Howard Jarvis Taxpayers Association, joined the group later. Chuck Betz served as president at the time Proposition 13 was put together. Leona Magidson served as secretary-treasurer, and offered her home as the organization's headquarters. There were countless others, including people who would join up with Jarvis from other parts of the state, like Joe Donohue and Ann Anger in San Jose, Les Kelting in San Mateo, Jane Nerpel, Ernie Dynda and Eunice McTyre in the San Fernando Valley and Lee Phelps from Santa Cruz.

In his book about the Proposition 13 story, *I'm Mad as Hell*, Jarvis remembered that when he spent all night on some talk radio show, he would give out Leona Magidson's phone number so people who couldn't call into the show could have their questions answered. "People would be calling her all night. Then she would spend all day addressing envelopes, stamping them, and stuffing them and sealing them. Leona has really been at the center of our operation."

Magidson said she put in the hard work because of Jarvis. "Howard Jarvis is the reason I stayed with it all these years. I just believed in him. I felt that any man who could do what he was doing for nothing, I could believe in. He was the first human being I had come across politically whom I thought cared."

More importantly for the taxpayer movement, Magidson said, "All of a sudden, we had a leader."

She could not have foreseen the battle that was beginning. It would take sixteen years and a lot of false starts and failed efforts before the property tax relief war would be won in California.

Early Tax Revolts

In his story, the legendary but fictional Zorro stood up for the people in Old Los Angeles against the cruel *alcalde* who subjected the people to unreasonable taxes. In truth, for the taxpayer, Spanish rule and early Mexican rule was what tax expert Dave Doerr characterized as the "Golden Age for the California Taxpayer."

In his extensive examination of California taxes in his book *California's Tax Machine*, Doerr notes that, "From 1769 to 1850 there was no system of direct taxation of real property in this territory." Most of the government revenue came from tariffs. Under Mexican rule, taxes soon were levied on alcoholic beverages, making the alcohol tax the most historic of all taxes Californians now pay.

The property tax was established by California's first legislature meeting in Monterey, known as "the legislature of 1,000 drinks." The first property tax on real and personal property was an annual one-half percent of assessed value as determined by the county assessor.

However, while taxation was established at the beginning of California statehood, so were the seeds of tax revolt.

As Doerr explains, in 1850, a five-dollar head tax was placed on every male inhabitant between the ages of 21 and 50. The purpose of the tax was to "ensure persons with no real and little personal property paid some amount for the benefits of state government." However, of the 10,299 miners assessed, only 716 paid, perhaps California's first tax revolt.

But property taxes, the chief reason for the Proposition 13 revolt years later, would cause great problems for the young state of California to the point of almost breaking it apart.

Gold mining created instant growth and a booming economy. When gold was first discovered, California's government was a military one, led by Colonel Richard B. Mason. Along with his aide, William Tecumseh Sherman, who would become a famous Union general during the Civil War, Mason went to visit the gold fields as soon as he learned of the discovery.

Mason pondered how to have government benefit from the activities of the miners and considered collecting fees or rents but, on reflection, decided to take a hands-off policy. He informed his superiors in Washington that the government and the people would benefit most from the gold mining if the workers were left unburdened by government revenue agents. Such enlightened leadership and economic vision has proved to be almost non-existent in government decision making.

Gold mining took place in northern California and the state legislature was very pro-miner, which brought on the first property tax crisis in the state. "Diggin's" on federal lands where the gold was were exempt from property tax, meaning the property tax burden fell on the counties to the south. By 1859, residents in these counties had had enough and they wanted to separate from northern California. The legislature allowed for a referendum on secession and it passed three to one. According to James Ring Adams in *Secrets of the Tax Revolt*, the reasons for the secession effort were too much taxation and not enough representation. However, when the request to create a new state was transferred to Washington, it got caught up in the tussle over the coming Civil War. No new state could be created in such an atmosphere, and once the war came, the request for a new state in southern California was forgotten.

It seems that tax revolutionaries and property tax protests were born with the state. The Gold Rush times are often described as "wild and wooly." But, there would be no more wilder and woollier time than that during the battle over Proposition 13.

"Never Give Up"

Concerns over high property taxes are sprinkled throughout California history. In the 1930s, government officials figured that it was better to replace the property tax on cars with a vehicle license fee because too often, when the owner of the car knew the assessor was coming to check it for assessment purposes, the owner simply drove the car away.

In the late 1950s, property tax increases rallied outraged protestors to a meeting in the Los Angeles Coliseum. Although the 6,000 protestors would have made a scene if crammed into a hotel ballroom or a meeting hall, they appeared insignificant in the cavernous football stadium. Radio and television broadcast legend George Putnam took part in that meeting and remembered how small the gathering looked in the big arena. "If you're going to impress people, for God's sake, put it in a small area so that it overwhelms the room."

But it was the decade prior to 1978's Proposition 13 that the action against the property tax really heated up. Howard Jarvis and his United Organizations of Taxpayers were on the scene and in the 1960s he made his first effort to qualify a ballot initiative to undo the property tax burden. His proposal: Eliminate the property tax and allow other taxes to make up the difference. Jarvis and his colleagues gathered only 100,000 signatures of the half-million he needed to put his proposal on the ballot.

Governor Hiram Johnson, who campaigned with the slogan "Kick the Southern Pacific Railroad out of the Legislature," added the ballot initiative process to the California Constitution in 1911. In the early decade of the twentieth century, the Legislature was under the influence of the Southern Pacific Railroad. To break the railroad's monopoly on the Legislature, Johnson wanted to give the people a way to make laws when the Legislature failed them. Johnson was elected governor in 1910 and a year later, the ballot initiative process was added to the State Constitution by a vote of the people in a special election.

To qualify an initiative for the ballot, signatures of registered voters needed to be gathered on official petitions containing the measure. For an amendment to the State Constitution, the number of signatures required was equivalent to 8% of the number of all voters who voted for governor in the previous election. To qualify an initiative statute for the ballot, the required number of signatures was 5% of all gubernatorial voters. The signatures had to be collected in 150 days.

Signature collection is not an easy task. Howard Jarvis would try four times to qualify a property tax limitation measure before he would be successful, each time getting more signatures than the time before; each time educating more Californians about the problem of rising property taxes.

While Jarvis failed to qualify his initiative in 1968, another property tax reform measure did qualify. Surprisingly, the author was no less than the assessor of Los Angeles County, Phil Watson. Well, maybe it was not so surprising. By following the law and annually jacking up taxes, Watson was subject to vitriolic abuse from those who suffered at the hands of the taxman.

During Watson's term of office, the cost of homes went up steadily. Los Angeles County was so large it was difficult to assess all the properties each year. If a home had not been reassessed for a couple of years, when the assessor finally got around to recording the new assessment, the new value put on the property would result in a whopping tax increase, shocking the taxpayer. In accord with state law, the assessor raised the values, and therefore the taxes, to what was determined to be the "highest and best use" of the real property. If a small home stood near an apartment complex and the land the home was situated on was zoned for an apartment building, the assessor would put a value on the land as if an apartment building occupied that spot.

One only can imagine what happened to a retired couple who faced the ruinous tax increase reported by the *Newhall Signal* in 1966. Because they lived on land near a new apartment house, their small home was valued at an amount requiring them to pay taxes of $1800 a year. The total income of this retired couple was $1900 a year.

Dramatic property tax increases were imposed in the mid-1960s. Property tax protests broke out in many parts of the state. In part, the tax increases were the result of the Legislature's response to assessor bribery scandals in San Francisco and elsewhere. Bribes were used to keep assessments low. In some cases, consultants worked in cahoots with an assessor. The consultant would help a client lower an assessment set too high by the assessor, then the consultant would split the fees received for getting the tax reduced with the corrupt assessor. When these schemes were uncovered, the assessors of San Francisco and Alameda Counties were convicted of bribery and sent to prison, and the San Diego County assessor committed suicide.

The Legislature passed a law mandating that assessments be equalized and brought up to full market value on a regular schedule. Because this law hit at time of rapidly increasing home prices, taxes jumped up. Soon bumper stickers appeared in San Francisco pleading: "Bring back the crooked assessor."

Jarvis joined forces in supporting Phil Watson's initiative in 1968 but the measure was handily defeated at the polls by more than a two-to-one vote.

Watson qualified a second initiative to reform the property taxes in 1972. This measure, Proposition 14, also failed at the polls by a similar two-to-one margin.

One of the opponents of Watson's second measure was California's governor, Ronald Reagan. Reagan, who would support Proposition 13 a decade later, had an alternative tax reform plan that would also control spending, which he thought was superior to the Watson proposal. In a December 1972 postmortem review of the recent election, Lawrence Fisher from the Public Relations firm Braun and Co. wrote, " Governor Reagan's proposal of an alternative tax plan during the closing weeks of the campaign was instrumental in convincing the voters that they had another option rather than voting for Proposition 14. His continuing outspoken opposition right up to election day was a key factor in changing the minds of many voters."

True to his word, Reagan brought forth his tax reform measure the next year as Proposition 1. He worked closely with Lew Uhler, who would later run the National Tax Limitation Committee. For property taxpayers, Proposition 1 assured them that the local tax rate would not exceed present levels although there were some exceptions.

Howard Jarvis supported Proposition 1. He became

part of the official "Yes" campaign speaking on its behalf. According to campaign records at the Reagan Presidential Library, Jarvis spoke to a number of Republican groups, and also addressed members of the Fresno Apartment Owners Association and users of the Long Beach Jewish Community Center just days before the election.

However, Proposition 1 met the same fate as the Watson initiatives. It was defeated, but by a much closer margin, 54%–46%.

The property tax situation for homeowners continued to get worse. According to the Real Estate Research Council of Southern California, between 1972 and 1977, home prices in southern California doubled. Even if tax rates didn't change (and L. A. County Supervisor Kenneth Hahn would always brag that there was 'no tax rate increase'), property taxes doubled over that time based on increased assessments alone. The tax increases were made more jarring for taxpayers if their property had not been reassessed for a few years. They got hit all at once with a huge increase in taxes based on greatly increased property values.

A number of bills were introduced in the Legislature to try to slow down the rapid tax increases. One was modeled after a plan in place to reduce tax rates when school assessments increased, schools already being the driving force behind dramatic tax increases. But all these legislative remedies failed and the property tax pain continued to intensify.

The year before Proposition 13 made the ballot, the Legislature made one last effort to solve what everyone in Sacramento realized was the number one problem in the state: out-of-control property taxes. Dave Doerr, who was chief consultant to the Assembly Revenue and Taxation Committee at the time, wrote that the key reason for the failure of that effort was "abandonment of the principle of across-the-board property tax relief. Proponents turned the property tax relief package . . . into a vehicle for income redistribution. In addition, the proposal was too complex."

With another failure by the Legislature to solve the

problem, the door now was open to Howard Jarvis. He had tried to qualify a property tax relief measure four times, falling 400,000 signatures short the first time, 100,000 signatures short on the second effort, 10,000 short the next time and only 1,400 signatures short the last time. The man whose motto was "Never give up" would not fail again.

"Don't give them the money in the first place"

Signs of tax revolt were all around. Many people in these post-Watergate years of the mid—to late 1970s were disillusioned with government. When Ralph Peck wrote the *Long Beach Independent* in 1976 protesting that his Whittier home's taxes more than doubled in one year, he argued, "I'm not anti-government. I'm a flag-waver. But I speak up when I feel I should. Most people are afraid of government but they shouldn't be."

For those people who were afraid to speak up, they had a champion in Howard Jarvis. He continued to travel the state, speaking to audiences large and small, convincing people that the property tax system must be changed. Estelle Jarvis said, "If anybody was talking about property taxes, Howard wanted to go to the meetings and I always went with him."

As early as 1970, the *Los Angels Times* acknowledged that Jarvis was a taxpayer leader, "the chief spokesman for a large group of disgruntled California property owners who are convinced, simply, that they pay too much of the cost of government."

Jarvis used the relatively new programming format of talk radio to get his message out. He was a regular visitor on three highly rated Los Angeles radio programs hosted by George Putnam, Hilly Rose, and Ray Briem.

The Briem show ran overnight on KABC radio. At times, Jarvis would sit in for the entire five hours of the program talking taxes. The interest he generated, more than anything else, indicates how hot the tax issue was and how peeved the taxpayers were—five straight hours of angry talk about taxes in the wee hours of the morning!

Government representatives tried to calm down the angry taxpayers but got more than they bargained for. B. T. Collins represented Governor Jerry Brown in a debate with Howard Jarvis at San Marcos High School near Santa Barbara in 1976. Collins was a charismatic Vietnam veteran who wore a hook in place of the hand that he lost in the war. Later, he served as a Republican Assembly member. Two thousand people showed up for the debate. Collins had a rough day with the hostile crowd. He was hooted during his remarks. A picture in the *Santa Barbara News-Press* accompanying the story of the debate shows a bemused Jarvis looking up at Collins as he tries to make his argument to the hostile audience. Jarvis was on the warpath that day suggesting to the crowd that if the situation didn't improve, they should consider not paying their property taxes.

The taxpayer pain did not improve. Jarvis complained that politicians would raise assessed value one year, the tax rate the next year and the loser was always the same— the taxpayer. Politicians would complain that they just were following the law when they raised assessments and that they could not do anything about it.

Veteran San Francisco budget analyst Harvey Rose remembered the tax-and-spend process before Proposition 13 changed the way government did business. He told the *San Francisco Chronicle*: "Before Proposition 13, the mayor had a relatively easy job. You added up all your revenues and all your expenditures, then ... you just socked it to the taxpayers."

Jarvis would come up with ways to demonstrate that taxpayer money was wasted while people were desperately trying to hold on to their homes. For instance, he filed a suit in 1971 over the Los Angeles County Board of Supervisors underwriting a visit to Los Angeles by the New York City Opera. He wondered why the taxpayers should bear this cost when "maybe one-tenth of one percent of the taxpayers were interested in opera."

He could not countenance the county paying for youngsters to sing and dance while taxpayers were losing their homes. His case was dismissed.

And the taxes kept climbing.

In a July 14, 1977 editorial in both the morning *Long Beach Independent* and evening *Press Telegram*, the paper complained that the newly announced property taxes would go up as much as 107%. "The cost of government per person hasn't increased 107% in the past year," the editorial pointed out. "Neither is the owner of that piece of property getting a 107% improvement in government services." The editorial went on: "Of course, as we have pointed out in prior editorials, high taxes are not caused by high assessment but how much government spends."

Howard Jarvis had a solution to too much spending. "The only way to control government spending is don't give them the money in the first place."

Gann

While Howard Jarvis was trying to qualify a property tax-cutting initiative in southern California, retired real estate agent Paul Gann was making a similar attempt in northern California. Neither man was successful although the combined total of signatures they had gathered separately would have been enough to qualify one unified measure for the ballot.

Gann was about a decade younger than Jarvis, more soft-spoken with the appearance, mannerism, and speaking style of a country preacher. He ran a small taxpayers group in the Sacramento area called People's Advocate.

Since Jarvis's last attempt to qualify an initiative failed by only 1,400 signatures, it was natural for him to link up with Gann to get more signatures in the north. But how Jarvis got together with Gann for the purposes of writing Proposition 13 became kind of a joke around the offices of the Howard Jarvis Taxpayers Association (HJTA).

(The organization, founded by Jarvis to protect Proposition 13 after it passed and to further the purposes of the tax revolt, was originally called the California Tax Reduction Movement. It was renamed to honor Jarvis in 1988, a couple of years after his death. For the purposes of clarity in this work, the organization will be referred to as the Howard Jarvis Taxpayers Association.)

Over the years, dozens and dozens of callers to the Jarvis office claimed they were responsible for getting Jarvis and Gann together. After getting such a phone call, the person who got the call, either HJTA Executive Director Kris Vosburgh, Administrative Assistant Ed Thomas, or I would report that the tally increased, and that the "real" person who got Jarvis and Gann together had just called.

According to Jarvis, the person who put Jarvis and Gann together was Los Angeles County Assessor Phil Watson. Watson's initiatives to reform the property tax had failed to pass but he was aware of the other efforts to qualify property tax reductions. When Watson and Jarvis finally decided to work on an initiative together, Watson brought Gann into the mix. All three had worked separately on property tax reform measures and it made sense that if they combined their efforts on a new measure, it could qualify for the ballot.

However, Phil Watson was in trouble. His office was being investigated for serious wrongdoing and Jarvis didn't want the investigation to cloud the initiative effort. Jarvis said the only way he would agree to sign as proponent of the new initiative was if Watson did not sign. Watson stepped back and Jarvis and Gann were the proponents of what became Proposition 13. Watson meanwhile resigned from office claiming stress on the job. He never was indicted for any wrongdoing.

According to then president of the United Organizations of Taxpayers, Chuck Betz, putting Jarvis and Gann together to create a tax relief plan did not go smoothly at first. Betz said after a particularly difficult session between Jarvis and Gann on George Putnam's radio show, extra meetings had to be called to clear up differences and smooth over personality conflicts. But with those problems resolved, Proposition 13 moved ahead with Jarvis and Gann as co-proponents of the measure.

The initiative that the proponents put together was succinct and direct. It limited property taxes to 1% of the full cash value of the property, less than the 1.5% that Gann previously had promoted. Gann, however, got his provision requiring a two-thirds vote for the legislature to raise any new state taxes. James Ring Adams wrote that Jarvis had been willing to substitute other taxes for the property taxes following Watson's lead. This tax replacement proposal was the same approach Jarvis had taken in his first initiative attempt that would have eliminated property taxes all together.

Jarvis and Gann added new provisions to the measure that neither one had sponsored before, rolling back taxes to the 1975–76 tax year, allowing for a 2% tax increase per year to cover inflation, and a new requirement calling for a two-thirds vote of the people to pass "special taxes" in local jurisdictions.

Unlike many initiatives, what became Proposition 13 fit neatly on one page. Jarvis said the language was simple because the purpose of the measure was simple: "In plain English, what we were trying to accomplish was to put a fence between the hogs and the swill bucket."

The measure would take about 500,000 valid signatures to qualify for the ballot. Jarvis figured that with Gann working northern California he finally would amass enough signatures to qualify his tax reform measure for the ballot. In the end, he did not need the help. Proposition 13 qualified with more signatures than any initiative in history up until that time—1.2 million. Truly a citizen's petition, the signatures were gathered by volunteers. Jarvis said the United Organizations of Taxpayers spent only $28,500 in qualifying the initiative, an amazingly low figure considering that initiative campaigns routinely spend a million dollars to make the California ballot.

For the first time, an initiative received signatures in every one of California's 58 counties. Gann delivered 158,000 signatures but Jarvis gathered more than a million. An additional 300,000 came in after it was too late to file them.

Jarvis and Gann split up after Proposition 13 passed. While there were difficult moments between them, they smoothed things over and worked together on a future tax-cutting measure. Jarvis praised Gann for helping to get signatures in every county and for doing what he said he would do to help get Proposition 13 on the ballot. At a Prop 13 tenth anniversary celebration in 1988, two years after Jarvis had passed away, Gann lamented having the celebration without his old compatriot, "It's hallelujah time again, but I sure miss Howard. Now some people hated us, that's true, but a lot more loved us."

After Gann passed away in 1989, his family started a new organization headed by his son, Richard Gann. Gann's assistant, Ted Costa, now ran People's Advocate. The new organization was called the Paul Gann's Citizens' Committee. In 2000, the family decided to merge the Committee into the Howard Jarvis Taxpayers Association so, in a sense, Gann signed up with Jarvis again to continue the fight for taxpayers.

It took many people across the state to make sure Proposition 13 made it to the ballot. And while Jarvis appreciated all of them, he had special praise for the woman who stuck with him through years of disappointment after disappointment—his wife Estelle. "Estelle worked as hard as anyone . . . and when Proposition 13 came along, she organized a crew of women to gather signatures. She would pick them up in her car every day, make their lunch, and take them to a supermarket where they stood outside and got people to sign our petitions. Her crew turned in about a thousand signatures a day, from September to November 1977."

Along with Estelle Jarvis, her sister Dolores Tuttle, who lived at the Jarvis home, also contributed to the difficult task of making the initiative drive succeed.

With the measure qualified for the June ballot, the political class took notice. Assembly Speaker Leo McCarthy called the 1% tax limit initiative a financial disaster for local government. Opponents began a campaign to disparage supporters of the initiative whom they called greedy and misguided.

Dorothy Dallas responded for a lot of taxpayers with a letter to the *Santa Monica Evening Outlook*: "I am one of the 1.2 million voters who worked to qualify the Gann-Jarvis Initiative. The reason I worked is to save my home, not to 'save money' as some of our opponents suggest."

But the political establishment was not afraid. They already had beaten Watson twice and Reagan once, the former an assessor of California's most populous county, and the latter a governor of America's most populous state. Surely, they could handle Jarvis and Gann. They were nobodies.

PART THREE

*The Proposition 13
Campaign*

The Campaign Begins

Assessing the combatants on both sides of the Proposition 13 campaign, not too many generals would want to lead the troops supporting the measure. The heavy artillery was on the other side.

Nearly the entire political establishment opposed Proposition 13: large majorities of elected officials from both parties, local government officials and the bureaucracies, public employees, businesses and business associations, most all of the media, many academics and other opinion leaders.

When General Jarvis looked behind him, all he saw were the people who were tired of being kicked around by government, not listened to by politicians, and scraping to pay their taxes. He was ready to take on the challenge. Jarvis later wrote:

> I guess nobody chose me to lead the parade. I guess I chose myself. If I hadn't done it, I don't think anybody else in California would have done it. Nobody. The proof of it is no one else did it.
>
> My taxes don't worry me. I'm worried about the guy who can't pay his taxes. That was one of the big advantages I had over anybody in politics: I had no axes to grind. I went up before an audience of 200 or 50 or 2,500 and I told 'em just what I felt. If they didn't like it, the hell with 'em. I wasn't running for a damn thing. Anybody out there that I talked to, there was nothing they could do for me.

What all these people were doing—if they did what
I asked them to—was helping themselves.
Whatever they did, they didn't do for me, because
I'm not going to get a penny out of it. All I was
doing was showing them how to help themselves.
But the politicians are afraid to tell the truth,
because they're afraid they'll lose votes. I don't
care whether I lose 4 votes or 4 million. If the people
were not smart enough to save their own necks after
I told them how, what else could I do?

So I kept plugging away. Estelle and many of
my friends wanted me to give up. I was working
my tail off and spending my own money, and for
most of that time, all I had to show for it was a bad
press. Their cartoons implied that I was a thief or a
nut or a fool. And so did their stories. But I had a
hell of a thick skin.

Like the ragtag soldiers at Valley Forge, the people
fighting for Proposition 13 would overcome terrific odds.
But then, that is the stuff of legends. There was a lot of
"We the People" in the Proposition 13 campaign. The
political experts and the establishment told people what
was good for them, that they didn't understand that the
remedy they backed for property tax reform—Prop 13—
was worse than the disease. Jarvis was convinced that the
goal of politicians was to make government so complicated
that the people would not understand it and would walk
away leaving the politicians a free hand.

But the politicians did not have all the answers either
and the people knew that to be true. They have known
about that political weakness since the country began. As
Jarvis said, "An election year is the time politicians promise
to get us out of the trouble they got us into in the first place."

The election in June 1978 would be different. It was
the voters' turn to get themselves out of the trouble that the

politicians had put them in. No matter what the odds against them.

Big Business

Surprising to some, the business community, especially big business, stood opposed to Proposition 13. Businesses did not just lend their names to the "NO on 13" campaign; they helped lead it and they supported it financially. The NO on 13 campaign was co-chaired by Howard Allen, ex-vice president of the Edison Co., and Walter Gerkin, chairman of the Board of Pacific Mutual Insurance, was the finance chairman.

Conrad C. Jamieson, vice-president of Security Pacific National Bank, was quoted in an anti-Prop 13 flyer saying, "(Proposition 13) would be like an atomic bomb exploding the whole tax structure ... The personal income tax, sales tax, corporation tax and all other taxes would have to be increased substantially to make up for it."

Pretty static economic thinking from a banker. The tax cut had the potential to stimulate the economy and bring in new tax revenues to government. That is precisely why then-USC economist Arthur Laffer supported Proposition 13. Already gaining fame as the creator of the Laffer Curve, which showed that tax rates increased beyond an optimum point would actually decrease revenue to government because the high taxes discourage work and business investment, Laffer said, " ... with property taxes lower, businesses will expand their activities within the state. This expansion will create new jobs, more investment, and higher real wages. Sales, incomes and other forms of activity will expand. Sales taxes, income taxes, etc., all will rise."

Well-known business associations like the California State Chamber of Commerce and the California Taxpayers

Association (Cal-Tax), a big business-supported taxpayers' group, campaigned against Proposition 13.

But while the business leadership opposed Proposition 13, the opposition was not very deep. Kirk West, who headed Cal-Tax at the time, told of speaking against Proposition 13 to a room full of business executives. He gave the pitch for a "No" vote on 13. When he was finished, the faces in his audience showed little enthusiasm so he asked for a show of hands, "Who is going to vote 'Yes' on Proposition 13?" Practically everyone in the room raised a hand.

Why so many business leaders and organizations opposed Proposition 13 is not clear. It could have been that they were afraid that open support of Proposition 13 would hurt their businesses at the hands of a vindictive governor, legislature or local government officials. Others might have bought into the argument that taxes would be raised to make up for fewer property tax dollars and that business would be the prime target for tax increases. However, this argument does not work when you consider that business supported Proposition 8 on the ballot put on by the Legislature to counter Proposition 13. Proposition 8 called for a modest property tax reduction on homes and a property tax increase on business.

Finally, businesses opposed to Proposition 13 may have been bought off by legislative action. The Legislature passed a bill signed by Governor Jerry Brown that allowed for phasing out of the business inventory tax. A tax was levied on business inventory in California every March. However, the bill stated it would only go into effect if Proposition 13 were defeated at the polls! (The business inventory tax was eliminated later even after Proposition 13 passed.)

No matter the reason major businesses opposed Proposition 13, practically all of them did. Howard Jarvis said, "Business's greatest inventory is political cowardice."

Business was used another way during the campaign

to convince voters to oppose the tax-cutting measure. Although business was helping the "NO" campaign, that campaign decided to use the negative stereotype of rich, greedy businesses to trawl for votes. The "NO" campaign pointed out that businesses would enjoy a great windfall if taxes were cut. It's true, at the time that Proposition 13 passed, that business (including residential property that was rented) received about two-thirds of the property tax cut, but that was because they paid two-thirds of the taxes.

Yet, the argument was made that Proposition 13 was designed to help big business. Jarvis called this charge a "lie because for more than fifty years, the state constitution has required that residential and business property be appraised, assessed, and taxed on exactly the same basis . . . Proposition 13 did not touch that formula, which is still in effect. So if Proposition 13 gave a windfall to business, it's the same old windfall the politicians have been giving to business for over half a century."

Tax expert Dave Doerr, then working for the Legislature and now with Cal-Tax, said the argument didn't work. "It was hard to convince the voter to give up $1,000 in property tax relief simply because some business was going to get more."

Over the past twenty-five years, many observers have remembered the situation the wrong way—they thought business supported Proposition 13. Lou Cannon, who covered Ronald Reagan in Sacramento then followed him to Washington and worked for the *Washington Post*, wrote a column about Proposition 13 in which he declared business was a supporter of the measure. He also wrote in another column that Proposition 13 was "of the selfish, by the selfish, and for the selfish." He was wrong on both counts. I sent him a copy of the campaign report showing that business financially opposed Proposition 13 by funding the "NO" campaign. I should have sent him all the letters from senior citizens that said "Thank you for saving my home."

Still, the falsehood persists that business supported the Prop 13 campaign. In 2002, when the San Fernando Valley was attempting to secede from the city of Los Angeles, the *Los Angeles Times* had a long article about how the secession movement was attempting to model itself politically after the Proposition 13 campaign. Even though the reporter researched that issue and discovered that business opposed Proposition 13, an editor insisted that he knew the truth because he was around at the time, and that business supported 13. That is how the story came out.

Perhaps the idea that business supported Proposition 13 continues because once the initiative passed, business used it as a sales tool. Kirk West, who became head of the state Chamber of Commerce, used to tell businesses considering moving into California that their property taxes would be settled and certain because of Proposition 13. In some states, property tax often is like a snake to business; it must be handled very carefully because it could bite. Property taxes often are set at the whim of the local assessor and can vary dramatically with similar properties. Having a set tax rate (1%) and a pre-determined yearly increase (2%), as provided for by Proposition 13, is a plus for any business looking to relocate or start-up.

In his book *Small Property Versus Big Government*, Professor Clarence Lo argued that big business secured the benefits of the tax revolt for themselves over the small-time activists who started the revolt. Despite those activists' general satisfaction with the results of the tax revolt, this argument may also lead to the mythology that business was behind Proposition 13.

In fact, Jarvis skillfully used the opposition of big business in his fight to pass Prop 13. He managed to lump big business together with other opponents who did not instill confidence in the average voter. "When you see politicians and bankers and union leaders standing together against something you're for," Jarvis said, "then you know that there's no way in the world that you can be wrong."

In recent years, many in big business have decided that more taxes are needed for schools, roads and other capital improvements in California and many business associations generally have supported these targeted kinds of tax increases. Most of these taxes do not fall heavily on business. After twenty-five years, a shift now is being detected: The property tax burden is falling more and more on homeowners. The cozy relationship that business has enjoyed with Proposition 13 soon could change because of business's new tax support attitude. Business may be forced to shoulder a larger share of the total property tax burden.

Scare Tactics

Political scientists will tell you that it is easier to get a "No" vote than a "Yes" vote for a ballot measure. A "No" vote seems safer to many voters. If a measure is defeated, the status quo remains and the old saying, "You're safer with the devil you know than the devil you don't" will convince voters to stay put. One way to make that devil you don't know appear even more frightening is to use scare tactics.

In their book, *The Tax Revolt*, Alvin Rabushka and Pauline Ryan of the Hoover Institution at Stanford University wrote: "One had to be living in California to fully experience the degree to which the voters were warned, intimidated, threatened, or bribed by the ever shriller hysteria, dishonesty, and hypocrisy of 13's opponents."

That may be an understatement. Safe to say a volume could be put together containing some of the Doomsday prophecies of what would happen in California if Proposition 13 passed.

The opposition tried to make Proposition 13 look like the traditional wolf in sheep's clothing, or as Ed Salzman, editor of the political magazine *California Journal*, creatively put it, "The measure is like an immature orange—dollar green on the outside and sour on the inside."

One of the main attacks against Proposition 13 was that even if your property taxes went down, other taxes would have to go up and you would be paying more taxes in the long run. Government officials and official government reports pushed this higher tax angle. The Assembly Revenue and Taxation Committee under Chairman Willie Brown issued a report that said, in part: "If the state taxes are increased to make up the loss of revenue to local government, homeowners will, in all probability, experience a net tax increase as they pay a smaller share of the total property tax than they do of other major taxes such as sales and income tax ..."

Senator Albert Rodda proposed a $5.25 billion state tax increase if Proposition 13 were to pass. *The Los Angeles Times* then used the Rodda bill to show that Proposition 13 provided less relief than Proposition 8, the legislative measure put on the ballot to entice the voters not to vote for Proposition 13.

The flip-side of this scare tactic, also used by the Prop 13 opponents, was that if property taxes did go down and taxes were not raised, then local government was going to be reduced drastically—or close down altogether.

John Fitzpatrick, assistant to the Board of Supervisors in El Dorado County, said, "If the initiative passes, we can probably move the entire county (operation) into the library's Quonset hut and auction off the new county building."

C. Erwin Piper, the chief administrative officer of the City of Los Angeles, saw Armageddon for his city: "We would be faced with nothing short of disaster. Approval of Proposition 13 would bring the city's operations to a complete halt."

Cities and counties prepared Doomsday budgets—and released them to the press—calling for cuts in services of 30%—40% and more. Los Angeles County claimed it would have to cut its fire protection 71%.

In San Francisco, the city library posted a sign that read: "NOTICE! If Proposition 13 passes on June 6, the San Francisco Public Library WILL CLOSE EFFECTIVE JUNE 30, 1978."

By the way, that notice was located in the old main library building in San Francisco, not the brand new library building the city now has.

A threat to public safety was part of the scare attack. The Hillside Strangler was stalking L.A., killing women, and leaving their bodies on hillsides around the city. A high-ranking police department official said the police department would have to close the major-crime unit in charge of investigating the Hillside Strangler case if Proposition 13 were to pass.

If that were not scary enough for the residents of Los Angeles, the California League of Cities estimated that the Los Angeles Police Department would have to layoff 2,249 police officers if Prop 13 passed. Presenting a specific number that is not rounded off seemed more realistic and therefore accurate. Scared yet?

The gambit about public employees losing their jobs was not only to scare the voters but to scare the public employees as well. Convincing public sector workers that they would lose their jobs meant a built-in group ready to oppose Proposition 13, to spread the anti-13 word and to offer campaign contributions. Public employees were the victims of the hysteria campaign just as much as the general public was. A general manager of public employees of Riverside County, Vic Hochee, summed up the concern when he said, "Where do you think the savings to the homeowners is going to come from? Probably right out of our hides!"

That's not to say the growing number of public employees was not a cause for concern. The number of employees growing faster than the population put pressure on the budget. Using State Employment Development Department statistics, Jarvis said that in 1950, there was 1 government employee for every 30 residents in California. In 1960, the ratio had become 1 employee to every 25 residents, and by the time Proposition 13 was on the ballot in 1978, it was 1 employee for every 15 residents.

But it wasn't only the public employees who were going to lose their jobs. In probably one of the more infamous reports of the campaign, UCLA's Graduate School of Management reported that 451,300 jobs, both public and private, would disappear if Proposition 13 passed. The report said unemployment would jump from 7.2% to more than 10% in a year.

The report was wrong and the numbers changed downward as the complex model used to reach those conclusions was adjusted. However, the initial conclusion was never forgotten. A number of years later, Larry Kimball, one of the UCLA professors who worked on the study, said that that prediction would probably get placed on his tombstone.

Not all public employees went for the scare tactics. Firefighters at Local 112 in Los Angeles voted two-to-one to support Proposition 13.

And, at a UCLA cafeteria a number of years after Proposition 13 passed, a conversation was taking place among some younger workers about Proposition 13, and a few disparaging remarks were made. An older worker at a different table wearing a UCLA employee badge interrupted, saying that if it wasn't for Proposition 13, she would have lost her home and that she was grateful to Mr. Jarvis.

A judge told a law class about his dilemma, remembered Kris Vosburgh, HJTA Executive Director. "He had been told that if Proposition 13 passed, as a public employee, he would probably lose his job. If it failed, he knew he would probably lose his home. He weighed the difficult choice. With a sly wink he told his students, 'Think I voted for it.'"

The "NO" campaign spent a lot of time scaring parents and students that Proposition 13 would hurt education. The objections to Prop 13 came from throughout the education establishment, starting from the top. Children often were recruited by educators to do their dirty work by picketing speaking appearances by Jarvis, even late at night, and writing notes that were distributed to the public. In one case, notes supposedly written by sixth graders urging a "No" vote on Prop 13 were stuffed under windshields of cars parked at a shopping mall. The local newspaper pointed out that the tone of the note indicated the children were put up to this political activity by their teachers.

Ross Johnson, who was running for an Assembly seat in Orange County as a supporter of Proposition 13, was in for quite a shock when he went to pick up his little girls at an after-school day care center one day. Johnson saw four kids on their big wheel bikes with handpainted signs attached to the bikes reading, "Vote No on 13" and "We don't want our teacher to lose her job."

Johnson told his daughters, "I just came from knocking on doors, asking for votes and telling the voters I wanted Proposition 13 to pass."

Johnson said his daughter Susan started crying because she said she didn't want him to lose the election. To calm her and her classmates, he hugged her, Johnson said, and told her she was entitled to her opinion.

Not only did Johnson win, in great part due to his support of Proposition 13, he is now the dean of the State Senate.

Wilson Riles, the superintendent of Public Instruction, said Proposition 13 would decimate the schools. "Let's say

I have a headache. You do not solve that by cutting off one's head. That is the Jarvis approach to financing."

Apparently, the Riles approach to the agony of being taxed out of your home was to compare that life-altering event to a headache.

To put pressure on the teachers, school board members said that under state law, if teachers might be laid off the following school year, they had to receive official notification a few months before. Some of the school boards, including the Los Angeles school board, sent out the notices. L. A. Teachers Union President Hank Springer immediately held a press conference, tore up his notice, and said the teachers would flood the courts with lawsuits if they were laid off.

One of the great myths accompanying Proposition 13 is that California schools get less money today than they did when Proposition 13 passed. Not true. Despite incredible growth in student population because of births and immigration, both from other states and other countries, California today spends more money per pupil in inflation-adjusted dollars than it did in 1978. The school establishment never has answered satisfactorily how the money is spent.

While the scare tactics campaign was proceeding, politicians were attempting to use their power to manipulate the political process to give themselves an advantage over the supporters of Prop 13.

Powerful Assemblyman Willie Brown suggested that cities be rewarded or punished by either awarding or withholding state funds, depending how a city's voters voted on Proposition 13. If a city voted against Proposition 13, it would receive more money from the state.

"Pure and simple blackmail," Jarvis called it. He wasn't alone. The *Berkeley Gazette* editorial of May 23, 1978 stated, "Such a precedent would be dangerous as well as foolish."

In Los Angeles, County Supervisor Kenneth Hahn tried to get the assessor to freeze property tax assessments for the year so the voters of Los Angeles would not see a tax increase on their bills before they went to the polls. This would have been an illegal act on the part of the assessor and he did not comply.

Some, even in government, acknowledged the mean and dirty campaign against Proposition 13.

Napa County Administrator Albert Haberger said, "In all my years, I have never been so embarrassed as by such scare tactics. They were blatant and dishonest. We never did envision any great problems and had faith the state would help out."

A couple of newspapers were more blunt. The May 24, 1978, *Los Angeles Herald Examiner* declared that opponents of Proposition 13 had "stooped so low on a number of occasions that some of them need a hook-and-ladder to see over the curb."

And, the *Glendora Press* admonished a week earlier: "Holier-than-thou Democrats and bureaucrats are making Richard Nixon's Watergate scandal look like child's games when compared with the dirty tricks being pulled against Prop. 13 . . ."

With all the attempts to scare the voters, the campaign against Prop 13 failed, and failed big. Despite it being easier to get a "No" vote when uncertainty about the future is the chief attack of a campaign, the measure got nearly a 65% "Yes" vote.

Someone once said that in American politics, nothing much happens until the status quo becomes more painful than change. Certainly, that was the case with Proposition 13. The change might mean uncertainty and inconvenience, but the status quo meant cutting back, or personal debt, or losing your home. Under such circumstances, the people remained strong and heroic against all the false charges and scary scenarios thrown at them.

One Lonely Street Sign

Proposition 13 gave the opportunity for voters to voice their complaints about poor government service. Consider the contents of Mrs. R. L. Graham's letter appearing in the *Long Beach Press-Telegram* and her frustration over one "lonely" street sign.

The first day, she began, a city crew of two men came by her house and dug a hole. On the second day, they came back and brought a metal pole. On the third day, they put cement around the pole, and on the fourth day, they attached a sign saying streets would be swept on Wednesday.

But that wasn't the end. On the fifth day, they returned— and replaced the sign. Street sweeping was really on Tuesday!

Mrs. Graham closed her letter by stating she was voting for Proposition 13.

Norman I. Arnold wrote to the *San Francisco Chronicle*: " . . . We are saying that we know (Proposition 13) will severely disrupt state and city governments. We are also saying that we want it to severely disrupt state and city governments. We are not anarchists, we are not radicals, and we do not think we are irresponsible. We are simply fully sick and tired of having our pockets picked at every level of government . . . We want an end to the countless layers of useless bureaucracies. We refuse to pay any longer for the parasites who are feathering their own nests directly out of our pockets."

Presumably, Mr. Arnold voted for Proposition 13, too.

Ross Johnson in campaigning for the Assembly said, "I talked to thousands of people when I was campaigning. They brought up most the waste of money by the federal government, the waste by the state government. Liberals say 13 was an assault on local government. It was a means for the people to send a message. Create economy of government at every level."

It also didn't hurt the "YES" campaign when officials blundered, reminding voters why they were so angry with government. The San Diego City Council announced a 53% boost of their salaries just three months prior to the vote.

Most elected officials opposed Proposition 13. Likewise, many economists opposed it. However, not all did. Three distinguished economists who supported Proposition 13 were Arthur Laffer, Neil Jacoby, and Nobel Prize winner Milton Friedman.

Friedman said, "Everyone knows that you simply do not get your money's worth for what you pay for government. If government has $7 billion less to spend, the public has $7 billion more to spend, and will spend it more wisely ..."

Howard Jarvis said pretty much the same thing, but in his own inimitable style: "Money is much better off in the hands of the average citizen than it is in the greedy hands of those who live off the public payroll."

Attacks and Threats

Howard Jarvis became the focus of attacks during the Proposition 13 campaign. His pugnacious nature – Jarvis actually was a boxer as a young man in Utah and had sparred with future heavyweight champion Jack Dempsey – caused him to fight back, hard.

One constant refrain was that Jarvis, as executive director of the Apartment Association of Greater Los Angeles, had written Proposition 13 for apartment owners, in general, and himself in particular, because he would get rich when taxes were cut on all the apartment buildings he owned. The problem with this argument was that Jarvis did not own any apartment buildings, but the story persisted for years after Proposition 13 passed.

Assembly Speaker Leo McCarthy called Proposition 13, "The Apartment Owners Enrichment Act."

Jarvis debated McCarthy often, and in one encounter on the NBC station in San Francisco, McCarthy raised the apartment association issue. Jarvis hit back saying he was writing property tax reduction measures well before he worked for the Apartment Association, but that McCarthy was "running with real dirty money," the thousands of dollars donated each year by the public employee unions. Jarvis said, "They bought him and they own him."

Trevor Grimm, the Howard Jarvis Taxpayers Association general counsel, held the same position for the Apartment Association of Greater Los Angeles. Primarily, the Association was made up of mom-and-pop operations, and not big corporations. Grimm was aware of Jarvis's bulldog tenacity when dealing with elected officials and when the Association was looking for a new executive director in 1973, Grimm decided to see if Jarvis was interested.

At the meeting with the search committee, Grimm said Jarvis listened quietly while the dimensions of the job were described then asked boldly, "Who handles the money?" When he was told, "You do," he responded, "okay."

Then Grimm said Jarvis was asked how much money he wanted to do the job. "How much have you got?" Jarvis asked. "Not much," was the reply. Jarvis said, "I'll take it," and the deal was done. Jarvis recognized that the association would be a good platform to continue his crusade for property tax reform.

The issue of apartments and rents would remain an ongoing theme during the campaign. Jarvis predicted that rents would go down after the election if Proposition 13 passed because apartment owners would pass some of their savings on to renters. A number of owners did rebate either all or a portion of their tax savings to their tenants immediately after Proposition 13 passed. However, when new workers were drawn to the state by the economic upsurge, rents increased as the demand for apartments increased. In response to the higher rents, a number of communities, including Santa Monica and Los Angeles, enacted rent controls. Grimm said Proposition 13 was "used as a whipping boy" during the efforts to secure rent control.

In a debate at a Cal-Tax conference in the early 1990s, when Proposition 13 was being challenged on constitutional grounds before the United States Supreme Court, I faced off with a lawyer for the woman who brought the suit against Prop 13. The lawyer argued that the situation of similar homes next to each other paying different taxes because of Proposition 13's reassessment only on sale rule was unconstitutional as a violation of equal protection of the laws. She said it was not fair that one neighbor paid different rates than another for the same property.

I responded, "You mean, when a rent-controlled apartment is decontrolled, it's unfair that the neighbor who lives next door and remains in the building gets to keep the lower rent?"

She was silent for a moment then said quietly, "I don't have to answer that." And she knew that she lost the point, then and there.

Jarvis quickly discovered his time in the spotlight would result in personal attacks on him. In some cases, the threats were more serious than verbal attacks. He endured a number of death threats. They came both by mail and by phone. Jarvis took a number of precautions including occasionally hiring a bodyguard, putting metal mesh screens on his house, putting an alarm under the hood of his car, and even checking under the car for explosives.

Jarvis was not afraid to stand up and make his case, strongly and loudly. And that brought him enemies. The known enemies he could handle; it was the unknown ones who made him apprehensive.

But, he refused to be silenced. In fact, even after the death threats started, he declined to get an unlisted phone number. He was available to anyone who wanted to talk to him. They just had to look up his number in the book and dial.

The Media

Only one major state newspaper editorial page supported Proposition 13, the *Los Angeles Herald Examiner*. Now, it turns out, the *Herald Examiner's* support was phony. Apparently, the *Herald Examiner's* editorial position was offered not because the editors believed in the position they took, but because of competition with the *Los Angeles Times*, a higher calling for some editors than expressing their true feelings in print.

Jim Bellows, long-time editor of the *Washington Star*, *New York Herald Tribune*, and *Los Angeles Herald Examiner* recently published his memoirs. While on his book tour in Los Angeles, a *Los Angeles Times* reporter asked Bellows about his support for Proposition 13, which seemed incongruous with his liberal politics.

In *The Times* article published April 14, 2002, Bellows said the reason he supported Proposition 13 was "because the monster was against it," the monster being the *Los Angeles Times*. "And you don't mimic the monster. The underdog paper must distinguish itself every way it can."

When asked by the *Times* writer if that raised a question of integrity, Bellows answered, "I had to get people talking."

Now that this truth has been revealed, the fact is that no major newspaper editorial page actually supported Proposition 13. Newspaper editorials probably have influence with voters when complex issues are involved, or when little-known candidates are running for low-profile offices. However, the voters knew and understood what Proposition 13 was all about and newspaper editorial support did not matter.

Still, the media is an important part of any political campaign. To use an old adage: "You can't live with them and you can't live without them." The media broadcasts your arguments to a wide audience but also sends messages, both overtly and covertly, that can hurt a campaign.

California's leading newspaper in circulation and influence, the *Los Angeles Times*, vehemently opposed Proposition 13. The *Times* kept up an editorial drumbeat against the measure. On April 30, 1978, an editorial declared that if Prop 13 passed, Los Angeles County would eliminate all its paramedic units and close half of its fire stations. It would close half its libraries and 300,000 county employees would lose their jobs. The City of Los Angeles would cut thousands of police officers and firefighters and close many stations. More than 18,000 teachers would lose their jobs and students would go to school only half days.

Nostradamus had a better prognosticating record.

While these predictions might have come from simply subtracting the tax cut amounts from city and county budgets, a week later, the *Times* took another shot at Prop 13 by editorial trickery. Howard Jarvis described the suspect editorial in his book, *I'm Mad as Hell*:

> In an editorial on May 7 headlined "Deceit on the Schools," the *Times* quoted from the state constitution as follows: "'There shall be apportioned to each school district in each fiscal year . . . $120 per pupil in average daily attendance in the district during the next preceding fiscal year.'"

Take a close look at those three dots between the words "year" and "$120." Those dots are very important.

The *Times* went on to say: "That limit is the state's *only* (italics theirs) constitutional obligation to the districts ... Nothing in the Constitution requires the state to enlarge its present contribution of $120 per pupil if there is a decline in *local* (italics theirs) revenues for the schools, as there would be under Proposition 13.

The *Times* was trying to accuse Proposition 13 of potentially crippling the schools. They were attempting to make the point that we were lying when we cited the constitutional requirement that the state provide funds to the school districts as proof that 13 would not have such drastic effects on the needed school programs.

Let's talk about lies. Let's provide the three words between "year" and "$120" in the state constitution that the *Times* chose to leave out and replace with three dots. The three missing words are "not less than"!

What the constitution actually says is: "There shall be apportioned to each school district in each fiscal year *not less than* (italics added) $120 per pupil."

The *Times'* premeditated omission changed the meaning of the constitutional provision it cited so that it sounded as if $120 was the *maximum* the state had to provide to the schools, when in fact $120 is the *minimum*.

For Howard Jarvis, "*The Los Angeles Times* is the enemy of the people."

But Jarvis clearly was angry with the *Times'* management. He said, "The *Times* reporters who wrote about 13 generally wrote accurate and balanced stories. It's the same thing as what we ran into with big labor and big business: the average working guy gave us a much fairer shake than the fat cats did."

And, it was not only the *Los Angeles Times* that took shots at Prop 13 and Howard Jarvis. On March 31, the *San Diego Union* attacked with relish: "Proposition 13 is the difference between putting a mechanic to work on an engine that's out of tune, and giving a chimpanzee a hammer to beat on it until it falls apart . . . Proposition 13 is an unvarnished piece of demagoguery . . ."

And, of course, there were other editorials and even news stories that accepted the line of Proposition 13's opponents and bashed away.

Prop 13 supporters complained to the newspapers and some bought space in newspapers to counter the print attacks. The battle still was going on years later. Homeowner, Tommy Munoz, bought a quarter-page ad in the *Modesto Bee* to complain about that paper's coverage of Proposition 13 at the time the initiative's constitutionality was being challenged before the courts in the early 1990s.

Similarly, in 1994, the Howard Jarvis Taxpayers Association bought a full-page ad in *Money* magazine to counter a lengthy, derogatory story by journalist Richard Reeves.

It must be pointed out that a number of newspapers did complain about the distortions of the "NO on 13" campaign, and others agreed that something must be done about outrageous property taxes. Most of the supportive editorials appeared in smaller circulation newspapers, however.

Jarvis was able to get his message across on talk radio programs, sitting by the hour, fielding questions from the audience and talking directly to the voters with no reporter to screen what was being said.

George Putnam, long-time television and radio

broadcaster whose colorful career went back to covering Franklin D. Roosevelt in the White House, gave Jarvis an open door to talk about Proposition 13. He remembered Jarvis appeared on his show for something like 52 straight days, and the audience loved it.

"He was a barker and a salesman," Putnam said with appreciation. "He had all the good qualities going for him on radio. People could tell a faker and he wasn't one. He had an earthiness to him. No elitism. Just eye to eye, down to earth."

When it comes to media, however, television is king in California. Reaching out and touching the mass of voters was more easily done on television, where personalities are more vivid and the viewer can measure sincerity more easily than the reader of a newspaper. Television gave Howard Jarvis an advantage.

In 1978, Proposition 13 was the big story. Politics was more important to television news directors then. The helicopter hovering above the freeway car chase had not yet been invented.

And, in the great populous southern California media market, Howard Jarvis became a star.

"He galvanized people's interest in the political process," said Bill Butcher, who along with partner Arnold Forde and Stu Mollrich of the Butcher-Forde Consulting firm, helped Jarvis run the YES campaign over the last 100 days.

Twenty-five years later, Butcher still marveled about the amount of time that television news directors gave up to feature debates on this one political issue. "Every night for weeks, Channel 7 (ABC in Los Angeles) gave up 5 or 10 minutes to have Howard debate an opponent from the 'NO' campaign. ABC didn't do this out of the goodness of its heart. There was incredible interest from the public. I don't think a network station would offer presidential candidates a debate every night of the week today."

Butcher said that the opposition could supply anyone they wanted to debate Jarvis and that it usually was a different person every night: politicians, special interest representatives, union officials, or a business association representative.

"You got the feeling every night that Channel 7 was saying, 'Here's the world champion and here's his next challenger.'"

Butcher felt Jarvis's success on the debates, as well as with other appearances, was because he came across as refreshingly honest, something viewers were not used to in political debates. "People liked Howard. They knew he wasn't a slick-talking political suit. He could connect to the average person."

In the end, Jarvis's greatest satisfaction came when his political adversaries in the press admitted they were wrong.

One year after Proposition 13 passed, the *San Jose Mercury* editorialized:

> Just a little over a year ago, most California politicians, bureaucrats and newspapers—including this one—were opposing Proposition 13.
>
> We said it would cripple local government. When it didn't happen last year, the doomsday chorus said just wait, the ax will fall next year.
>
> Well, now it's next year. We've been watching San Jose's City Council put the finishing touches on a budget for fiscal 1979–80. And we have to admit, Armageddon is not exactly upon us. Looking at what Howard Jarvis's brainchild has wrought at San Jose City Hall, we see some things we don't like. But we also see some things we do like.

The Browns and the "Behr Trap"

Jerry Brown was California's governor when Proposition 13 was on the ballot. The son of former Governor Pat Brown and a rising political star, he was only 40 years old. Brown should have been a natural supporting Proposition 13 since he prided himself on having a good populist sense. When Brown first met Jarvis in "about 1968," Brown remembered suggesting to Jarvis that, "he cut property taxes just for homeowners, but Howard didn't agree." Brown talked about an era of limits, drove around in an old Plymouth and slept in a small apartment near the capitol. A man this frugal should have embraced Proposition 13, but he didn't.

Brown was the initiative's most visible opponent. He declared that the Jarvis measure would be "the biggest can of worms the state has ever faced." Governor Brown argued that local revenue losses could not be made up for by the state, and local government would suffer.

However, it was Jerry Brown's father, Pat Brown, who created a greater stir in the campaign when he sent out a short two-sentence letter on the letterhead of his law firm. It stated in its entirety, "If I were a Communist and wanted to destroy this country, I would support the Jarvis amendment. Your fellow Republicans who waffle on it should be impeached."

Jarvis called Brown's remark an insult, especially to the hundreds of thousands of Brown's fellow Democrats who signed the Proposition 13 petitions.

The *Los Angeles Times*, no friend of Jarvis, also was harsh on the former governor. His remark was "nonsense, and the senior Brown must know it . . . To suggest that Red legions are waiting to take advantage of it (Proposition 13) is plain silly."

Ironically, Jarvis, too, wanted to raise the specter of Communists in the campaign. He wanted people to know Communists opposed Proposition 13. Campaign consultant Bill Butcher said one of the things he spent time on was trying to convince Jarvis not to play the Communist card. Butcher said the voters would not see teachers and firefighters, who were speaking up for the "NO" campaign, as Communists.

Butcher's efforts were mostly successful. However, at one television debate, Jarvis suddenly whipped out a newspaper and showed its headline to the cameras. He had proof from a Communist publication that they did oppose Proposition 13. This incident did not get the publicity that the Pat Brown quote did.

Politicians decided they needed to offer the voters an alternative to Proposition 13 if they were going to defeat it. Governor Brown had called for a $1 billion homeowner and renter's tax relief package in his January State of the State speech. The legislative "alternative" came from the Senate, authored by Senator Peter Behr. Those who didn't like its provisions called the measure a "Behr Trap."

Behr's bill would become Proposition 8 on the ballot. It proposed to do a number of things to achieve some homeowner property tax relief and renter relief, but it only would go into effect if Proposition 13 were defeated. One main feature was a split property tax roll for business and residential property. It also contained a complicated tax growth control mechanism that according to tax expert and former Assembly Revenue and Taxation Committee consultant, Dave Doerr, probably would have worked against the measure's touted intentions and would have forced taxes to increase during the inflationary years of 1979 and 1980. Suffice it to say, like most government solutions that try to satisfy many interests, Proposition 8 was complicated and unwieldy. KNXT-TV (CBS Los Angeles) reporter Bob Dunn probably spoke for a lot of people when he told the *Los Angeles Times*, days before the election, "I have difficulty in understanding it."

Jerry Brown agreed. Twenty-five years later, when asked what could have been done to derail Proposition 13, Brown quickly answered, "We needed a better alternative sooner. The alternative we offered was too complicated. Howard came along and just cut 7 billion, gave the money to the people. It was simple."

However, the "YES" campaign perceived Proposition 8 as a threat. "We were fearful at first when the legislature put it on the ballot," said Butcher. "But then we realized it wasn't working. Voters thought it was phony. People were angry about Prop 8. In the end, it hurt them (the 'NO on 13' campaign)."

But, the Prop 8 campaign brought forth a new challenger to debate Jarvis. Senator Behr was now out in the field supporting his measure and attacking Proposition 13. In a debate before the prestigious Commonwealth Club of San Francisco, Behr called Proposition 13 "fiscal heroin."

Jarvis took the high road in response. "The purpose of a free country is to enrich the country and not the bureaucrats . . . Personal freedom is absolutely and intimately intertwined with economic freedom," Jarvis said.

"If You Want to Send a Politician to Paris, Vote No."

The "NO on 13" campaign, backed by big business, wealthy unions, and politicians, tied into solicitous lobbyists, did raise more money than the "YES" campaign. However, the difference was not great—about $200,000.

The remarkable thing was, with the help of Butcher-Forde and their direct mail efforts, the "YES" campaign was able to keep up with the big money players with small donations of $5, or $10 from overburdened homeowners and retired folks on fixed incomes.

Only one five-figure contribution came into the "YES on 13" campaign—a $16,000 donation from Jarvis's own employer, the Apartment Association of Greater Los Angeles. There were only a couple of four-figure donations. However, the "NO" campaign swept up the cash in horse-choking rolls. The California Teachers Association and its affiliates gave $225,000. The California State Employees Association added $100,000. A group of brokerage firms that sold municipal bonds added $125,000. There were other large donations as well.

The purpose for this money was to reach voters through ads. Both sides relied on mail and radio ads, as well as newspaper ads. Individual taxpayers and local taxpayer groups not associated with Jarvis's main campaign often sponsored small newspaper ads in local newspapers. The "NO" campaign could afford large ads signed by important people opposing Proposition 13.

On radio, the "NO" campaign ran a commercial that informed listeners that seven past presidents of the American Economic Association as well as 450 economists teaching at California's universities and state and community colleges all opposed Proposition 13 because they felt it would have a terrible effect on the California economy.

The "YES on 13" side was on the radio, too. Former governor Ronald Reagan voiced one ad running statewide. The theme of the ad was preserving home ownership as a piece of the American Dream. Former Los Angeles Police Chief Ed Davis, then running for the Republican nomination for governor, voiced an ad played in the Los Angeles media market countering attacks that public safety would be hurt if Prop 13 passed.

However, it was on TV where the battle would be won or lost.

While Jarvis spoke in some ads, campaign consultant Bill Butcher said the most effective ad the pro-Proposition 13 forces ran was "boring." It simply had economist Milton Friedman on the screen reassuring viewers about Proposition 13.

Friedman said: "Don't let politicians fool you. Proposition 13 will work. It will not force schools to close. It will not cause policemen or firemen to disappear. It will not require increases in other taxes."

But, most important, said Butcher, were the words across the screen that identified Friedman as a "Nobel Prize–winning Economist."

"The people wanted to vote for 13, but they wanted to be sure the state wasn't going to hell in a hand basket," Butcher said. "People wanted to be reassured by someone they trusted." Added Stu Mollrich, who helped put together the Friedman ad for the Butcher-Forde firm, "Howard was under attack from experts. By having a Nobel Prize winner, we put a lid on the hacks raising doubts."

The "NO" side's television ads featured firefighters and teachers asking for a "No" vote on Proposition 13. "The opposition ran a good campaign," Butcher said. "It was the same campaign that beat Reagan and Watson (initiatives). The ads focused on fear of losing police, and fire and schools. We had to focus the voters on the greater fear of higher taxes and losing their homes rather than the fear of government collapse."

The television ad that got the most attention had little to do with property taxes. The ad started with an airplane taking off. Then there were still shots of resorts and landmarks around the world. The ad copy read, "Each year, California politicians go on expensive junkets all over the world, stay at expensive hotels and hand taxpayers the bill. Your Yes vote on Proposition 13 will force an end to this kind of wasteful government spending." Over a picture of the Eiffel Tower dissolving away to be replaced by an airplane the voice over concluded, "But—if you want to send a politician to Paris, Vote No."

As the plane disappeared, words on the screen were spoken by a different voice: "Cut your property taxes by two-thirds. Show the politicians who's boss. Vote Yes on 13."

Butcher said he and Forde and Mollrich discussed if using the words "Vote No" would backfire but, in the end, decided the viewers would get it. Mollrich said, "We would be concerned with the words 'Vote No' if it were not a well-publicized campaign. But people knew what 13 was about."

The opposition squawked about the commercial, which got the ad even more attention. And, the complaint crystallized a legitimate antipathy for wasteful government spending.

Purveyors of Dishonesty and Hypocrisy

The campaign to defeat Proposition 13 was starting to work. A hail of negative arrows carrying uncertainty and doubt were hitting their marks. Voters were getting nervous about what the future might bring if they approved a dramatic tax-cutting measure. Like most initiatives, the strong initial support Proposition 13 enjoyed before the attacks against it began was now weakening in the polls.

However, two events occurred in the month before election day that turned those polls around and sent Proposition 13 to an overwhelming victory. One was the affirmation that the state of California was sitting on a huge surplus of taxpayer dollars that could be used to offset the tax cuts. The second was the release of tax estimates in Los Angeles County that confirmed what Howard Jarvis was saying all along—property taxes would continue to soar.

The state of California adjusts its budget revenue estimates in May after tax returns from April are counted. This activity is called the May revision or simply the "May revise."

In May of 1978, the revise reported that the budget surplus was around $6 billion dollars. The state budget that year was around $15 billion. That means the state government had been collecting taxes at a phenomenal rate, enough to have a 40% surplus, while legislators were fiddling with tax relief proposals and homeowners were burning, wondering how they were going to make their property tax payments.

News of the surplus, which State Treasurer Jesse Unruh called "obscene," made the voters angry. Ross Johnson heard a lot about the surplus when he went door to door campaigning for his assembly seat. "People weren't angry at city and county government. They were angry about the $6 billion surplus in the state. They heard a lot about it."

News of the surplus sent shockwaves through the "NO" campaign. All along, they had argued that public services would collapse without the property tax money and now came proof that there was adequate money in the state to fund government services. While some would argue that the surplus was state money and the property tax cut would be lost to local government, as HJTA Executive Director Kris Vosburgh later would say, taxpayers understood that all taxes are personal—they all come from the same taxpayers' wallets, no matter what their final destination.

The huge surplus also confirmed another fact for the voters—government was getting too big. State spending had increased over the last few years but tax revenue was coming in faster and even government could not spend it all. Or, as Howard Jarvis said, "We had given the politicians and bureaucrats an unlimited budget and they had exceeded it."

Howard Jarvis spent the campaign reminding voters how quickly the property tax had increased over the years and he emphasized that those taxes would continue to go up. Campaign consultant Bill Butcher said this tax-increase argument was a main strategy of the campaign.

"The key to a win was getting Howard to talk about how much people's taxes would escalate. Howard would say if you don't pass Prop 13, your taxes would go up 50%. Later (in the campaign), he would push it up to 100%. Then later, we wanted him to say taxes would triple. We were hoping an assessor or someone on the other side would break and say, 'No, Jarvis is wrong, taxes won't triple, they're only going to *double!*' Then we had them. We never expected it would be the assessor of Los Angeles County that would do it."

Alexander Pope had been appointed Los Angeles County assessor when Phil Watson resigned. He was new to the job and was running for election on his own right in November and he did not want to be accused of hiding tax increase bills before the June primary election. He opened up records that indicated many homes in Los Angeles County were facing a 100% increase in their property taxes.

The uproar over the new tax increases could be heard from the Oregon border to the Mexican border. In Los Angeles County, the supervisors tried to get Pope to rescind the increased assessments. Governor Brown saw an opportunity to squelch the screaming about tax increases and asked all state assessors to freeze assessments.

However, the State Board of Equalization, an obscure but elected board that oversees taxes in the state, stepped in and said freezing assessments on a whim was illegal.

Property taxes now were certain to go up, many as high

as 100% unless Proposition 13 passed. Howard Jarvis had been right all along.

The "YES on 13" campaign quickly acted to score points with the newest revelation. As Stu Mollrich described the ad he put together, "A jack-in-the-box was on the screen and there was the slow grinding of the music that we all associate with a jack-in-the-box. The voice-over said 'Politicians have a surprise for you after the election.' The box pops open and Jack is holding a sign that says: Property Taxes up 300%. And the voice says: 'Surprise.'"

"It was great," said Mollrich.

Alvin Rabushka and Pauline Ryan summed up the disastrous situation for the "NO" campaign in their book, *Tax Revolt*: "All along, the opponents of 13 had said that government could not function without the property taxes. Now, they were taking politically motivated action to stop increases in these 'essential' revenues. Between the surplus and the Pope affair, Jarvis emerged as a champion of integrity and government officials as purveyors of dishonesty and hypocrisy."

"The Message of Proposition 13 Is Clear"

In the May 23, 1978, *Esquire* magazine, journalist Richard Reeves wrote, "Most knowledgeable Californians are predicting that the amendment (Proposition 13) will be defeated." In retrospect, this statement is reminiscent of *New Yorker* magazine movie critic Pauline Kael's famous line when she could not understand how Richard Nixon defeated George McGovern for president: "I don't know a single person who voted for him."

I guess it depends on whom you talk to. The "knowledgeable" elites Reeves talked to were in the dark.

Others were making different predictions. Gubernatorial candidate Ed Davis predicted the Jarvis tax limitation initiative would sweep the country and become part of every state constitution in 10 years.

Well, you might say that Davis's prediction was closer than Reeves' but it also missed the mark.

Hitting a bull's-eye as a prognosticator was Jarvis. He told the *Sacramento Bee* on May 29, more than a week before the election, that Proposition 13 would pass 65% to 35%.

On election day the final tally read:

Proposition 13

Yes	4,280,689	64.8%
No	2,326,167	35.2%

Proposition 13 lost in only three of California's 58 counties: San Francisco, no surprise; Kern, by 650 votes out of 92,000 cast; and Yolo, which houses many state workers who commute to Sacramento and is a small community that contains a large University of California campus. The turnout for a primary election was the highest in 20 years.

On election night, June 6, 1978, Howard Jarvis celebrated at Los Angeles's Biltmore Hotel. He noted the significance of the date, the same as D-Day when the Allies stormed Hitler's Fortress Europe in 1944, and concluded the impossible dream by saying the people were now in control. David had slain Goliath. People could and did control their government.

"The message of Proposition 13 is clear," Jarvis told a packed ballroom. "Government must be limited. We have a new revolution against arrogant politicians and the insensitive bureaucrats who love to tax, tax, tax; spend, spend, spend; and elect, elect, elect. This is bankrupting us, the American people, and the time has come to put an end to it."

The momentous occasion was not lost on the national media. The tax revolt story became the rage. Proposition 13 was the cover story in both *Time* and *Newsweek*.

From *Time*:

> That sound roaring out of the West—what was it? A California earthquake? A Pacific tidal wave threatening to sweep across the country? Literally it was neither, figuratively, it was both. That angry noise was the sound of a middle-class tax revolt erupting and its tremors are shaking public officials from Sacramento to Washington, D.C.

From *Newsweek*:

> Defying the counsel of politicians, labor leaders and economists, a damn-it-all 65% of the voters backed a proposal to slash their own property taxes—and made Tax Revolt the new gut issue in American politics . . . The California tax revolt had raced the middle-class pulse of the country as feverishly as anything since the invention of the station wagon.

From *U.S. News and World Report*:

> Taxpayers throughout the U.S. are sending a message to city halls, state houses, and Washington, "Roll back spending and cut our taxes."

From *Barrons*:

> We feel on safe ground when we predict that this particular California earthquake will register on political Richter scales around the nation.

From the *New York Times*:

> (Prop 13) is the leading edge of a political storm
> of taxpayer revolt this year.

More than a month after Proposition 13 passed, President Jimmy Carter said, "I think there are lessons to be learned from Proposition 13. I think the passage of Proposition 13 has sent a shock wave through the consciousness of every public servant—presidents, governors, mayors, state legislators, members of Congress . . . I do believe that Proposition 13 is an accurate expression of, first of all, the distrust of government. I'd like to restore that trust."

One political cartoon at the time showed a fat politician astride a horse with the Washington monument and the capitol in the background and the politician was yelling: "The taxpayers are coming! The taxpayers are coming!"

Proposition 13 had struck a deep chord. *Newsweek* even reported on June 26, 1978, "One analysis showed that 43% of government workers in California voted for Proposition 13—even though some of them were bound to lose their jobs . . ."

"Proposition 13 passed because it had to," said Marin County Assessor/Recorder James J. Dal Bon at a 1990 speech to the Commonwealth Club. "The legislature was doing nothing. There was no relief to aid property taxpayers. They were being asked to carry an inordinate burden. So we had a revolution."

In his book, *Secrets of the Tax Revolt*, James Ring Adams, marveled five years after the victory: "Even writing so close to the event, one constantly marvels that such a thing could have been done with such success. Yet this phenomenon is part and parcel of all the other wonders of California's history."

The legend had begun.

PART FOUR

The Immediate Aftermath

Civilization As We Know It Has Not Come to a Sudden Halt

Proposition 13 was the law of California, the talk of the nation, and Howard Jarvis was a media star. That kind of power had great sway in the political world. Not only would Jarvis make the rounds of national talk shows; make an appearance in the movie, *Airplane*; see a board game produced titled "Ax Your Tax" featuring his picture; accept an offer to write a book by a division of the New York Times Book Service; be honored with the Golden Plate Award from the National Academy of Achievement, the Thomas Jefferson Award and Daniel Webster Award, and receive one of four runner-up positions as *Time's* Man of the Year, but even Tom Hayden came to visit.

Hayden, the political opposite from Jarvis, a '60s radical who had lost a U.S. Senate Democratic primary race a couple of years before, was about to launch a political career in the California legislature. One witness at the meeting described it as a friendly conversation about what Proposition 13 meant to the state and its populist attraction to the voters.

However, Jarvis would use his influence in electing Republicans to office. Teaming up with supporters of Proposition 13 and working with Allan Hoffenblum, who was directing political efforts for the state Republican Party, many letters were sent out supporting pro-Prop 13 candidates.

Hoffenblum remembered that one of the candidates for Assembly, Dennis Brown, came to see him with some interesting polling information. Brown's poll consisted of two questions. The first question asked how voters intended to vote in his race. The answers showed that newcomer Brown was substantially behind. The second question asked, "If you knew that Dennis Brown supported Proposition 13 and his opponent opposed it, how would you vote?" The numbers nearly flip-flopped. Hoffenblum decided to poll other districts using similar questions. The results were nearly the same.

Hoffenblum sought out Jarvis and put together letters in sixteen races, including the State Senate, the Assembly and Congress, all tailored to each particular race. Jarvis's letters stated simply that the Republican newcomer had supported Proposition 13 and that the Democratic incumbent had opposed it. The letters hit just a few days before the election and caught the incumbents off guard.

Fourteen of sixteen incumbents opposed by Jarvis were defeated. Pro-Prop 13 Republicans elected to the legislature for the first time were dubbed "Proposition 13 babies." Hoffenblum said, "It was the biggest election landslide for California Republicans since the election of Warren Harding."

Prior to the November general election, the Legislature had jumped on the tax-cutting bandwagon by chopping a billion dollars off of state tax bills. All the measures adding up to this billion-dollar tax cut passed unanimously.

The Legislature was responsible for implementing Proposition 13, which meant moving the huge state surplus to local governments to fill in for the tax cuts. Dave Doerr described a "charged meeting of the Assembly Democratic Caucus, some members opposed implementation, under a let-the-blood-flow-in-the-streets theory to validate the arguments used by the opposition." However, cooler heads prevailed.

The so-called bail-out to help local governments took the form of block grants to local governments, with the state assuming the cost of certain county responsibilities such as Medi-Cal. But it must be remembered that this state money came from the same place as the local money that was being replaced—it all came from the same taxpayers. If some reorganization had to occur to satisfy the requirement of reducing the property tax to save homes, that was fine with the taxpayers.

There always are loose ends when dramatic changes occur in government operations, but revolution is done with a broadsword, not a scalpel. As former *Wall Street Journal* writer James Ring Adams wrote, "In cutting the Gordian knot of public-sector spending, they took an approach as brutal and direct as Alexander's, and left as many frayed ends. Yet, they successfully reversed the state's pattern of rapidly increasing tax burdens."

The bailout went relatively smoothly in protecting local governments and Proposition 13's tax cuts did the rest, stimulating the economy.

Fortune magazine ran an article a year after Prop 13 passed titled, "Proposition 13's Stellar First Year."

Economist Arthur Laffer studied the California economy and said, "In the aftermath of Prop 13's passing, California outperformed the rest of the nation in nearly every conceivable measure including personal income growth, employment growth, and real estate appreciation values."

While state and local property tax revenues fell, higher revenues in other categories largely offset them. Local government direct expenditures hardly declined. The tax reduction, which had invigorated the state's economy so profoundly, imposed no significant reduction in government services. If anything, Proposition 13 and other tax limitation and tax reduction measures which soon followed, benefited California's private sector and California's public sector by giving incentives to workers to earn and keep more money and help the economy grow. Tax revenue increased as a result of this economic growth. The California tax revolt of the late 1970s more than paid for itself.

The tax revolution was gaining respect from opponents, perhaps in part because of the movement's political power.

Leo McCarthy, who so vocally opposed Proposition 13, a year later signed a ballot argument for Paul Gann's spending limit initiative. He wrote, "No government should have an unrestricted right to spend the taxpayers' money. Government should be subject to fiscal discipline no less than the citizens it represents."

And nearly seven months after Proposition 13 passed, on the pages of the *Los Angeles Times*, L. A. City Council member Marvin Braude wrote:

> Those of us who opposed Proposition 13 have a problem. Now that the measure has been in effect almost six months, how d o we account for the fact that civilization, as we know it has not come to a sudden halt? . . . We, who thought that Proposition 13 could not, would not (perhaps even must not) work, were simply wrong. We, public administrators, officials, those whose interests are closely tied to public spending—in short, we in the governing class—made a fundamental if all-too-human error in confusing our own convenience and welfare with the people's interest.

But not all were jumping on the bandwagon and not everyone was a fan of Howard Jarvis. The *Boston Globe* reported on February 10, 1980, that a newspaper columnist suggested that workers at San Francisco City Hall run an informal popularity poll matching Howard Jarvis and Leonid Brezhnev, ruler of the USSR. They did and Brezhnev won. But then again, it was in San Francisco.

Proposition 13 Around the World

Howard Jarvis took little time taking his tax-cutting message to the nation's capital. He had such a small boy's wonder about him that this kid from a little mining town in Utah was featured on *Meet the Press*. Also, he found that, despite his victory only a few days before, he still was debating the issues on the show.

Jarvis went on to the Washington Press Club to spread the word of tax revolt. He said, "We're not going to permit the people to go broke while the government gets rich. It's them or us, and we're for us."

Nobel Prize–winning economist Milton Friedman also sensed a national trend brewing over tax cuts. "The sweeping victory of Proposition 13 will be heard throughout the land. The 'brewing' tax revolt is no longer brewing. It is boiling over ... The public refused to be bamboozled this time, as they had been so often before ... The populace is coming to realize that throwing government money at problems has a way of making them worse, not better."

In an August 1979 radio commentary, Ronald Reagan referred to a *New York Times* article citing 22 states that cut property taxes in the wake of Proposition 13. That number would climb to 43 states that cut or reformed property taxes because of what happened in California.

President Carter, who said there were lessons to be learned from the tax revolt, also sloughed off the vote as an aberration brought on by unique circumstances in California. Congress, however, decided to call a hearing about this amazing idea that people actually wanted to cut their taxes.

UCLA economist Neil Jacoby testified in front of the subcommittee of the U.S. House of Representatives Banking, Finance and Urban Affairs Committee, telling the members that taxpayers were better off spending their own money. The Congressional members apparently didn't want to hear that message. The subcommittee report said, "We have identified Proposition 13 as an event which, unless understood and properly responded to, could do serious damage to the federal system."

Congress was looking out for its own skin, afraid the tax revolt would spread to its doorstep. And, it would, in the very next presidential election.

Proposition 13 also received worldwide attention. At the creation of the Taxpayers Association International in Washington, D.C. in September 1988, Eric Risstrom of Australia told a news conference, "We thought we were alone until we heard of the California Tax Revolt." A representative of a Portugal taxpayer group proudly showed off a letter he received from Howard Jarvis.

Jarvis met with Margaret Thatcher in London to talk taxes. In the Howard Jarvis Taxpayers Association office in Los Angeles is a framed copy of a British editorial cartoon showing Jarvis as the Statue of Liberty.

On a fact-finding tour to the U.S., 19 members of the Swedish Parliament met with Jarvis. Afterward, he commented, "My message to them was to cut taxes, but they won't. They're getting too fat living off someone else's labor to worry about the fate of their country."

But the message of Proposition 13 was being heard far beyond California's borders.

Jerry Jarvis

As election day for Proposition 13 neared, Governor Jerry Brown could see the handwriting on the wall. Proposition 13 was going to pass. He pulled back on his criticism of the ballot measure, and after election day, the governor, like any good leader, jumped in front of the parade.

"We have our marching orders from the people," Brown said. "This is the strongest expression of the democratic process in a decade. Things will never be the same."

Brown now cast Proposition 13 as a "great opportunity" to make government work more efficiently.

The governor already was thinking of implementing Proposition 13. Howard Jarvis often told the story of Brown visiting him not too long before the election, unannounced. Jarvis was home with the flu and answered the door in his pajamas. The governor wanted to chat, so Jarvis invited him in, threw on a robe and sat talking to him for hours. They talked about the state surplus that was in the news and the local government surpluses that did not get any publicity. They talked about property taxes, how best to use them, and how not to use them. Estelle Jarvis came home and made them lunch, but only after scolding Howard for sitting around with the governor of California in his robe over his pajamas and no shoes and no socks.

That unannounced visit was not the only one Brown made to the Jarvis home. On another occasion, the governor knocked on the front door and Estelle's sister, Dolores, answered. Dolores resided in the home with Howard and Estelle. She was asked whether Howard was home. "No," she replied. The man at the door explained he was the governor of California and asked if it would be all right if he and his assistant waited inside for Howard to return. "No," Dolores replied, and that was that. So much for unannounced visits.

Brown went to work implementing the will of the people by trimming the state budget and freezing state employee salaries, but he did more than that. He set out to change his image and the public perception of him when it came to Proposition 13. *Newsweek* quoted an unnamed Brown critic that, "Within a month you'll think it was Brown's proposition."

Sure enough, less than a month after the election, a *Los Angeles Times* poll showed that a majority of the people polled believed Brown had supported Proposition 13. Brown's quick changeover from opponent to cheerleader for Proposition 13 earned him the nickname "Jerry Jarvis." One of the few political cartoons that Jarvis had hanging in his office was a series of five inked headshots—the first one on the left was of Jerry Brown and over the course of the five pictures the headshot altered until the final picture on the right had morphed completely into a perfect Howard Jarvis.

But the morphing went both ways. Howard Jarvis was moving in a direction he never went before—voting for a Democrat for a top office.

Jarvis cut a television commercial for the Republican candidate for governor, Attorney General Evelle Younger, praising him for his strong defense of Proposition 13 before the California Supreme Court. But then, he also made a commercial for Brown saying he was taking the right steps to cut state spending and implementing Proposition 13.

Asked to defend how he supported two candidates for the same office at the same time, Jarvis said, "Easily and in good conscience. Both of these candidates say they favor tax reduction and that is my target."

Gray Davis, now California's governor but chief of staff

to Jerry Brown in 1978, a number of years later told me about the filming of the campaign ad for Brown. Jarvis was reading off cue cards and had done a couple of takes reading that, "Paul Gann and I" wrote Proposition 13 but it takes a dedicated governor to make it work, then praised Brown. Davis said Jarvis seemed uncomfortable with the copy and asked to change it. Davis was worried that he would limit the praise for the governor. Jarvis walked over to the cue card with a black marker, crossed out "Paul Gann and," returned to his mark and smoothly read: "I wrote Proposition 13 ..."

During the campaign, Evelle Younger made a commercial showing a washing machine agitator bouncing Brown back and forth, attempting to show Brown flip-flopping on Proposition 13. However, what Younger saw as a weakness, voters saw as a strength. As Brown said, the people gave him his marching orders.

On election day in November, Howard Jarvis voted to re-elect Jerry Brown as governor. Jarvis was not turning his back on the Republican Party. In that same election, he helped put many Republicans into office. But, he said: "I couldn't walk around Brown. In the final analysis, after he promised me he would do everything he could to make 13 work, which is what he had been doing for the five months since 13 passed, and when I knew Younger did not have a commitment to 13, I had to vote for Brown."

Brown won, but the relationship between Brown and Jarvis began to sour. Brown not only took off the pay freeze for state employees but he offered them back wages. Jarvis thought this was an unconstitutional gift of public funds and sued. Jarvis lost, 6 to 1 in the California Supreme Court. "Don't you think they deserve it?" asked Supreme Court Justice Stanley Mosk.

Brown also came out against Jarvis's next two initiatives to cut the state income taxes in half, which lost, and to index the state income taxes to inflation, which won.

Brown decided to give up the governor's job in 1982 and he ran for the United States Senate against San Diego Mayor Pete Wilson. One day, Brown was in Los Angeles and called Jarvis in his office asking if he could drop in. Brown asked Jarvis if he would criticize Wilson for making an investment which looked like a tax dodge. Jarvis refused to help.

Brown was defeated by Wilson. The Governor's straightforward analysis was that maybe the voters were tired of him—and maybe he was tired of them, too.

When Brown lost the election to Wilson, Jarvis was tough on the governor. He was riled up about Brown opposing the latest Jarvis initiative, Proposition 7, to index the income tax. Jarvis wrote of Brown, "No governor in our state's history . . . has been so destructive. From all-out opposition to Proposition 13 and Proposition 7, to hundreds of millions wasted on the unnecessary med fly disaster (a fruit-fly infestation), Jerry Brown did all wrong. Good riddance!"

Yet, over the years, listening to Jarvis, even after the 1982 election, you could hear affection in his voice when he talked about Jerry Brown.

Amador

Even before the vote on Proposition 13, public sector lawyers were scheming as to how they could invalidate the measure in court. Actually, two lawsuits were filed before the election.

Ventura County Public Defender Richard Erwin tried to keep Proposition 13 off the ballot. He said Prop 13 would bring "anarchy" to state government. His lawsuit declared that the tax cut would limit funds to the public defender's office, therefore, his office would not be able to defend

indigent clients adequately, thus denying them constitutional guarantees to a proper defense.

A second lawsuit was filed by former Orange County Judge Bruce Sumner who said Proposition 13 violated the state constitution's single-subject rule. Initiatives are limited to only one subject and Sumner and others felt that Proposition 13 exceeded that provision by reducing property taxes as well as establishing vote requirements for tax increases in the legislature and at the local level.

Both cases were tossed out before the vote. However, once Proposition 13 passed, challenging it in court became the last remaining weapon for its opponents.

As early as April 1978, county attorneys began mapping strategy to attack Proposition 13 should it pass. The strategy suggested that more sympathy could attach to the case if it was led by a school district. The Amador Valley Joint Union High School District in Alameda County became the lead district, and the constitutional challenge to Proposition 13 became known as the *Amador* case.

Other school districts considered joining the case, and some did so. And, some school board members came to regret taking action against Proposition 13. In suburban Sacramento, the San Juan Unified School District school board members defied loud protests from taxpayers about using their tax dollars to challenge Proposition 13. They voted 4 to 1 to join the lawsuit. Immediately, taxpayers who just had successfully revolted against their high property taxes began a second campaign to kick out the four school board members who voted to join the suit. They gathered enough signatures for a recall vote and, on the general election ballot in November, all of the four school board members were booted off the board. The one person who voted not to sue and was not recalled was Dave Doerr, then chief consultant to the Assembly Revenue and Taxation Committee.

The California Supreme Court acted quickly on the *Amador* case so any legal doubts about the revolutionary tax-cutting measure could be put aside. The lawsuit challenged Proposition 13 on violating the single-subject rule, as Judge Sumner had attempted to do prior to the election; on violating the prohibition against an initiative revising the Constitution instead of amending it; on impairment of contract since the tax cut would require local government to forgo its contractual obligations that it could no longer afford; and, most significantly, it was claimed that equal protection of the law was violated because under the Proposition 13 system, side-by-side homes which were identical would pay different tax amounts depending on when the homes were purchased.

As a reminder: Proposition 13 created a new acquisition-value base for property taxation replacing the traditional current market value tax system. Instead of taxes being set by the tax rate being applied to the property's current market value as determined by the assessor, Proposition 13 declared the property's value to be the 1975-76 tax year's assessment value. The value only could increase up to 2% a year unless the property was sold or improved. When sold, the assessment value would be reset to the market value at the time of sale, most likely the selling price, and Proposition 13's 1% mandatory tax rate (exceeding 1% only for voter approved bonds) would be applied.

Under the acquisition formula, it was possible to have identical side-by-side homes paying different taxes depending on when the homes were purchased. This difference in taxation, opponents charged, violated equal protection of the laws because similarly situated properties were paying different tax amounts for the same services.

Attorney General Evelle Younger, arguing on behalf of Proposition 13, said if the court overturned 13, it "would represent nothing less than a statement by this court that the people of California have lost control of their government."

If the quip satirist Finley Peter Dunne created at the turn of the century were true—that the courts followed the election returns—then supporters of Proposition 13 had little to worry about.

On September 22, 1978, Howard Jarvis received a tremendous 75th birthday present when the California Supreme Court ruled that Proposition 13 was constitutional by a 6 to 1 vote.

The Court brushed aside challenges to the single-subject rule as well as the contention that the initiative was a revision to the constitution, declaring the measure operated "functionally within a relatively narrow range to accomplish a new system of taxation."

In other words, it was okay to require the Legislature to vote by two-thirds to raise new taxes, or to require a vote on local tax increases while reducing property taxes, because the people, by their vote on Proposition 13, were seeking tax relief. How in the world could you have tax relief if one tax was reduced while others were easily raised to offset the tax savings from the property tax cut? Setting up higher, more difficult obstacles to raise taxes would assure that tax relief would be a reality.

The Court pointed out that no contract was impaired explicitly by the Proposition 13 vote.

The only dissenting vote on Proposition 13's constitutionality came from Chief Justice Rose Elizabeth Bird on the question of equal protection. Justice Frank Richardson, writing for the majority, denied that Proposition 13 violated equal protection of the laws. "This acquisition-value approach to taxation finds reasonable support in a theory that the annual taxes which a property owner must pay should bear some rational relationship to the original cost of the property, rather than relate to an unforeseen, perhaps unduly inflated, current value. Not only does an acquisition value system enable each property owner to estimate with some assurance his future tax liability, but also the system may operate on a fairer basis than a current value approach ..."

There it was—the court recognized that revolutionary strength of Proposition 13. Voters would now have certainty about their taxes in having a set property tax rate (1%), in having a limit on assessment increases (2%), and in having a right to vote on future tax increases. All that, and the court said Prop 13 was fairer to boot.

On the point of equality, Richardson wrote that Prop 13 "does not discriminate against persons who acquired their property after 1975, for those persons are assessed and taxed in precisely the same manner as those who purchased in 1975, namely an acquisition value basis predicated on the owner's free and voluntary acts of purchase."

The reasoning is best understood if you look at home purchasers as if they belong to a college graduating class. There was the class of 1980, 1981, 1982 and so on. For people who purchased their homes all at the same time, say the class of 1980, similar homes would pay the same taxes because the market value would be the same. The market value might rise by 1982 so new purchasers would pay more in taxes than the persons who bought in 1980, but they would pay the same as neighbors who purchased their home in 1982, members of their same class.

This system has to be compared with what was going on in that same neighborhood before Proposition 13 passed. If one person bought a home at an inflated price, through no action of their own, all the neighbors would see their homes reassessed to reflect the inflated price and be taxed according to the tax rate set by the county. Many people could not afford that increase.

Over the years, many people complained about Proposition 13's acquisition tax system and about having to pay more taxes than their neighbors who lived in similar homes. However, many of those who complained, say in

1984 when they purchased their home, stopped complaining by 1986 when they realized that Proposition 13 was protecting them against wildly increasing property taxes.

It was on this equal protection issue that Chief Justice Bird dissented. Echoing the majority on the court, Howard Jarvis said, "Whether Rose Bird and other opponents of 13 want to admit it or not, there is nothing wrong with allowing a buyer to voluntarily determine his assessed valuation for tax purposes by deciding what to pay for the house."

Jarvis would join the successful effort to oust Rose Bird from the Supreme Court in 1984, in good part because of her vote against Proposition 13.

The United States Supreme Court turned down an appeal to hear the *Amador* case. However, the equal protection argument would continue to haunt Proposition 13 until a future U.S. Supreme Court decided to settle the question.

Estelle and Howard Jarvis

The winners. Election Night, June 6, 1978. Estelle Jarvis,
Paul Gann and Howard Jarvis (l. to r.) celebrate the victory
of Proposition 13. (credit: AP/Wide World Photos)

Current HJTA president Jon Coupal (at the microphone) leads a taxpayer coalition in opposing a ballot measure that would make it easier to raise property taxes.

Former California governor Jerry Brown addresses a meeting of the Jarvis Foundation years after Proposition 13 passed. (photo by John Barr)

The first Howard Jarvis Taxfighter Award. The award, a bust of Jarvis, is presented by Estelle Jarvis and Joel Fox to President Ronald Reagan. (photo by John Barr)

Jarvis goes to Washington. All of Washington was interested in the popular notion of tax cutting after Proposition 13's success at the polls. Here Howard Jarvis listens to a question surrounded by members of the United States Senate. Among those around the table are senators Sam Hayakawa, Bob Dole, Orrin Hatch, and Richard Schweiker.

Arthur Laffer, creator of the Laffer Curve economic theory and member of President Reagan's Board of Economic Advisors served as Chairman of the Howard Jarvis Taxpayers Association Board of Directors. (photo by John Barr)

Howard Jarvis joins California Governor George Deukmejian for a bill signing ceremony to protect property taxpayers.

To the Supreme Court. Then HJTA President Joel Fox surrounded by HJTA attorneys Jon Coupal (left) and Trevor Grimm in front of the United States Supreme Court building. Proposition 13's constitutionality was challenged in a case heard by the court. (photo by Michael Geissinger)

After the Supreme Court hearing, Joel Fox (second from left), Trevor Grimm (fourth from left), and Los Angeles County Assessor Kenneth Hahn (third from left) descend Supreme Court steps surrounded by reporters on the way to the microphones. (photo by Michael Geissinger)

Joel Fox talks to the media in front of the U.S. Supreme Court. On Fox's left is United States Senator John Seymour. On his right is Los Angeles County Assessor Kenneth Hahn and HJTA General Counsel Trevor Grimm. (photo by Michael Geissinger)

"All the headlines in the state." Joel Fox shows an audience the headlines from a number of California newspapers reporting that the United States Supreme Court ruled Proposition 13 constitutional. (photo by John Barr)

The Fisherman. Howard Jarvis was an outdoorsman, spending hours fishing in his favorite spot near Jackson Hole, Wyoming, or in the waters off of Canada (above).

"Don't Blame Proposition 13." A six-page ad signed by thousands of California taxpayers ran in the Sacramento Bee. (photo by John Barr)

Estelle Jarvis at a Tenth Anniversary of
Proposition 13 celebration.

To the ballot. Qualifying a tax reduction initiative for the ballot takes signatures from about a million Californians. Howard Jarvis holds some of the petitions from one of the measures he qualified on behalf of California taxpayers.

California Governor Pete Wilson, Joel Fox and Estelle Jarvis greet President George Bush at a meeting of the Howard Jarvis Taxpayers Association. (photo by John Barr)

HJTA president Jon Coupal speaks to a national taxpayers conference in 2001.

Jon Coupal, Dolores Tuttle, Estelle Jarvis's sister and member of the Board of Directors, Estelle Jarvis and Trevor Grimm in the HJTA offices.

HJTA supporter Arnold Schwarzenegger with HJTA Board of Directors and advisors.

PART FIVE

Proposition 13:
The First Shot in the Reagan
Revolution

Reagan and Jarvis from the Beginning

Proposition 13 and the presidency of Ronald Reagan are tied together like the moon and the tides. One had a mighty pull on the other. Proposition 13 would be to the Reagan Revolution what the Battles of Lexington and Concord were to the American Revolution. It was the first shot and it brought the issues of lower taxes and smaller government into clear focus, built up momentum, and steered the candidate toward victory.

Ronald Reagan's experience and instincts told him that high taxes discouraged productivity and hurt the economy. Reagan did not come to his war against high taxes when he was running for president. He had a long record of opposing taxes. Even his family members heard about his feelings toward taxes in a most personal way.

Son Michael Reagan told a story of asking his father for an increase in his allowance. Father Ron said he would gladly give his son an increase in his allowance—as soon as the government stopped taking so much money out of his paycheck. This was at the time that the movie actor was in the top tax bracket of over 90% before President John F. Kennedy cut taxes.

Pat Brown, Jerry's father, California's governor from 1959 to 1967, left office with the legacy of being a builder whose achievements included the intrastate water project and the California higher education system. While he accomplished these things during a period when California was collecting less tax revenue per capita than it does today, now, in the end, Pat Brown's administration was spending more money than it brought in.

Over the last three years of the Pat Brown administration, spending exceeded revenues. The deficits, however, were undisclosed by switching accounting practices to count revenue when it came due rather than when the revenue actually was in hand. When Pat Brown's successor, Ronald Reagan, moved into the governor's mansion, the deficits were waiting on the doorstep.

Reagan later calculated the state overspending figure at $1 million a day. This calculation underestimated the problem. Reagan felt he had been put in a box and was forced to raise taxes to deal with the huge deficit left by his predecessor. The new governor paid a political price for the tax hike. As I described it in a *Los Angeles Times* opinion piece on March 31, 1991:

> The year was 1968. It was opening day for California's newest major-league baseball team, the Oakland A's, freshly arrived from Kansas City. The fans were in a festive mood—until the dignitary was announced to throw out the ceremonial first pitch.
>
> Gov. Ronald Reagan was greeted with lusty boos timed by one reporter as lasting three minutes. After tossing out the pitch, Reagan commented, "I can certainly hear that a helluva lot of you paid your taxes."

With the tax spigot turned on, Reagan, himself, could not turn it off. His measure on the special election 1973 ballot to limit taxes and spending, Proposition 1, was defeated. Tax revenue continued pouring into the state treasury after the budget crisis was past. In fact, for the five years between the defeat of the Reagan initiative to

Proposition 13's tax revolt in 1978, state spending increased an amazing 12.5% a year and state revenues went up an incredible 18.4% a year. Tax revenue was coming in so fast, government couldn't spend it all!

When the voters overwhelmingly passed Proposition 13 in 1978, Reagan felt it reaffirmed what he wanted to do about cutting taxes on the federal level, according to advisor and now Hoover Institution economist, Martin Anderson.

The Proposition 13 victory fit perfectly with Reagan's own agenda of cutting taxes and stimulating the economy. "Proposition 13 was part of the ether, part of the air we breathed. It was there, we didn't have to talk about it," said Anderson who wrote Reagan's Policy Memorandum No. 1 for the 1980 campaign, which dealt with the economy and tax cuts.

As a political activist in Republican politics, Howard Jarvis had known Ronald Reagan for a long time. Jarvis had campaigned for Reagan's tax reform measure, Proposition 1, and had spoken on his behalf when he ran for governor of California in 1966 and 1970.

Jarvis even offered advice to the gubernatorial candidate on occasion. In a letter dated August 31, 1966, when Reagan was running for governor for the first time, Jarvis urged that Reagan put Governor Pat Brown on the defensive in the battle over Mexican American voters. Jarvis wrote that he had seen Governor Brown on television and that Brown said that farm labor jobs belonged to the Mexican Americans.

Jarvis continued: "If I were you, I'd be on the air at once charging that the Governor thinks that 'stoop' labor jobs are all the Mexican Americans should have and that his position on this relegates the Mexican American to this category, and really lets out of the bag what Gov. Brown really thinks. The Mexican Americans would then resent what Brown had said."

Jarvis went on to criticize Republican campaign

strategy. "One of the reasons the Democrats win is that they are so astute at seeing opportunities to hit back ... they don't wait days or even hours ... they do it while it's hot and while it's news. I believe that opportunities just like this one occur everyday and unless we hit them at once ... they never come back."

On September 7, Reagan responded: "I have been aware that in this period of getting reorganized, we have let some opportunities slip by. I'm going to take steps to correct this, and agree with you, the Governor must be on the defensive, and I'll have to put him there.

"I appreciate particularly your suggestion about the Mexican Americans and intend to use that in my own presentation in speeches, particularly in that community rather than just a press release."

True to his word, Reagan put Brown on the defensive; then on election day Reagan put Brown into retirement.

"Ronald Reagan for Proposition 13"

Finished with his second term as governor, Ronald Reagan set his sights on the White House. Taxes and spending would be one of the most important legs of the platform he would offer the American people. He often used taxes as a subject for his newspaper columns and for his influential syndicated radio commentaries in which he continued to tell the American people what he thought— indeed, what he was all about.

Not coincidentally, Reagan also often talked about freedom, but then the subjects of taxes and freedom are often related. Heavy taxes and too much government can reduce freedom. Reagan wanted to show the truth behind government rhetoric when it came to taxes.

Part of that truth, he believed, was that tax reform did not mean creating a more progressive tax system but making big, across-the-board tax cuts to stimulate the economy. In a March 1978 newspaper column, Reagan argued: "In Washington (and many state capitols), when the words are stripped away, 'tax reform' usually boils down to a little cut here, a little added there. The underlying assumption is that the cost of government can never go down, only up."

Reagan had embraced the work of economist Arthur Laffer by arguing (in a 1977 radio commentary) that, "government can increase its tax revenues and create the jobs we need without inflation by lowering the tax rates for business and individuals. We've tried spending our way to prosperity for four decades and it hasn't worked. If it did, New York City would be the most prosperous spot on earth. Twice in this century, in the 1920s and in the early '60s we cut taxes substantially and the benefit to the economy was substantial and immediate."

Reagan's attitude toward taxes since leaving the governor's office put him in a comfortable position to support the growing property tax revolt in his home state. Like many of his fellow Californians, property taxes were never popular with Ronald Reagan. More than once in his radio commentaries, Reagan liked to quote from polls showing the unpopularity of the property tax amongst the people. He thought property taxes hit the poor taxpayer with a triple whammy. In a commentary on November 2, 1976, Reagan complained that the dollars used to buy a home already had been taxed and did not receive the benefit of a homeowner's mortgage deduction. Then the home was hit with a high property tax, and finally inflation resulting from mismanagement of the budget and economy by the federal government would drive up the assessment of the home and property taxes would jump even higher.

When the battle over Proposition 13 was joined, Ronald Reagan was ready to enlist to defend the tax cut in both his radio program and his newspaper column.

In a radio broadcast on February 20, 1978, Reagan told his listeners: "If you live in California you know by now that the sky is scheduled to fall on June 6 ... Who do we have to thank for these timely warnings? None other than the good folks who brought you record-breaking public budgets, burgeoning bureaucracies and ever-higher taxes."

Later in that commentary, Reagan said, "Howard Jarvis, a 75-year-old veteran battler of high taxes stunned the spenders in Sacramento when his petition drive netted more than 1.2 million signatures—an all-time record."

Reagan didn't say so in the broadcast, but one of those signatures that put Proposition 13 on the ballot was his.

The former governor not only defended the initiative against outlandish attacks, he went on the offensive arguing the benefits of Proposition 13. In a speech before the Independent Petroleum Association of America in San Francisco two weeks before the election, the Associated Press reported Reagan said, Proposition 13 would "not only be beneficial to the business climate, but also to the people of California." He labeled as "scare talk" arguments that the proposition would cripple schools and municipal services.

A few days later (May 28, 1978), Bob Schmidt noted the similar approaches of Ronald Reagan and Howard Jarvis in a *Long Beach Press-Telegram* column: "Jarvis' contention about government greed and profligate spending is shared by other people, including Ronald Reagan. Reagan, when he was governor, used to say government budgeting should be like family budgeting. There is a finite amount of money, and spending should be confined to that amount."

Reagan's commitment to the Proposition 13 tax cut was on full display when he agreed to cut a radio commercial for the measure that ran statewide. After a narrator introduced the former governor: "Ronald Reagan for Proposition 13," that familiar, comfortable voice of the Great Communicator, said:

Home ownership is a big part of the American Dream. Yet, for millions of Californians, this dream is threatened or lost. Threatened by ever-rising property taxes. Property taxes which are already so high that many, especially the elderly, are losing their homes. Property taxes which are so high that renters must give up their dreams of someday owning their own homes. Property taxes that are so high that many must give up their hope of trading their house for that special dream home.

You have one last chance to protect the American Dream of home ownership. Vote Yes on Proposition 13—for the American Dream.

Fourteen years later, when Reagan addressed a meeting of the Howard Jarvis Taxpayers Association, he again displayed the essence of his philosophy when it came to tax-cutting—it was not merely about saving money: "As we pass along our hard-earned freedoms to each new generation, we must also pass along the will to fight to preserve them. When you and your fellow Californians passed Proposition 13 in 1978, you struck a powerful blow for freedom."

A Gadfly's Credo

Proposition 13 synchronized well with Ronald Reagan's thinking on taxes. What Proposition 13's success did was show him and his campaign team that the voters were thinking the same way, too.

"The idea of Reagan cutting taxes was now politically viable and rolling," said Martin Anderson, one of Reagan's economic advisors during the 1980 presidential campaign. "Proposition 13 was a clear political signal that the public was fed up with taxes."

Anderson said the vote on Proposition 13 was an important political event in the nation's biggest state and it was readily built into the campaign. "The idea of cutting taxes was no longer a theory. A referendum on cutting taxes had been put before the people and they supported it overwhelmingly."

Proposition 13's victory was the green light Reagan was hoping for in pushing his ideas on controlling federal taxes and spending. Limited government was a new mantra heard across the land. When Reagan talked about government being the problem instead of the solution, he knew he would have a receptive audience. Just as with the battles at Lexington and Concord, when citizens decided they would stand up against an unfair government with too much power over them, the Proposition 13 battle proved that the voters were willing to take a stand over bloated government and excessive taxation. Reagan, comfortable with that position, promoted it.

"Proposition 13 in California may be giving us one of those terms that become part of the language. *Prop 13* is becoming a symbol for citizen rebellion," he said on his nationally syndicated radio commentary taped July 15, 1978.

In his autobiography, *An American Life*, Reagan recalled Proposition 13 passing five years after the defeat of his Proposition 1, which he said was ahead of its time. "Now, people were rebelling, trying to get government off their back and out of their pocketbooks. That prairie fire I talked about was really spreading across the land, and it shouldn't have surprised anyone."

Reagan ratcheted up the rhetoric for federal tax cuts and continually reminded people of California's vote to show that a big federal tax cut could happen even if the current prospects for a federal tax cut were bleak. In a November radio commentary, noting that critics of the Kemp-Roth tax cut plan said the bill was dead, Reagan responded, "Kemp-Roth is not dead—ideas do not die, it is simply waiting for the wisdom of the people to be accepted by the majority in Congress."

The famous Reagan optimism was at work here. The tax cuts will happen; things will get better when congress finally listens to the people. And, the people had spoken loudly with Proposition 13.

Reading from a book written by legendary Treasury Secretary Andrew Mellon who served three presidents in the 1920s, Reagan showed his support for, and Mellon's presaging of, what would became known as supply-side economics. "What (tax) rates will bring in the largest revenue to the government, experience has not yet developed, but it is estimated that by cutting the surtaxes in half, the government, when the full effect of the reduction is felt, will receive more revenue at the lower rates of tax than it would have received at the higher rates."

Finally, Reagan showed how this theory could pay off by citing the John F. Kennedy tax cuts that resulted in "the longest, sustained economic expansion in the history of the country."

Reagan returned to the Kennedy tax cuts in future broadcasts to make this same point, capturing listeners' attention on a December 12, 1978 taped message with an against-the-grain comment: "Brace yourself. I would like to see the rich pay more tax." He explained that he wanted to secure more revenue from the highest tax brackets by cutting taxes and cited figures from the Kennedy years that a drop in the tax rate from 91% to 77% actually increased revenue in those tax brackets from $2.5 billion to $4 billion.

But selling the national tax cut agenda meant returning to Proposition 13 from time to time because that was the victory the people believed in and that was the foundation from which to discuss changes in the federal tax code. Reagan made the tie directly himself when he opened a radio commentary taped August 7, 1978: "It doesn't look as if Proposition 13 will go away as a conversation piece, or should I say the subject of taxes won't go away?"

In a commentary in February of 1979, Reagan called Proposition 13 "the first amazing shot in the nationwide tax revolt." It was the first shot in a revolt that had spread to other states. Reagan fully intended to take it all the way to Washington. The commentary was about a California state commission created by Governor Jerry Brown to look at implementing Proposition 13, a commission Reagan ridiculed for meeting to implement a tax decrease by recommending a tax increase! But even here, Reagan threw out a link to problems on the federal level when he said, "The big spenders in Sacramento—kissin' cousins to the ones in Washington . . ."

Proposition 13 not only set off a national debate for those who wanted to cut taxes and make government smaller versus those who fought for a bigger government, it also set off an internal debate among Republicans over tax cuts versus budget balancing. Reagan insisted you could do both, but he was convinced that cutting taxes was essential to spark the economy, producing more government revenue as a result.

UC Berkeley Professor Jack Citrin wrote, "Reagan quickly polished Jarvis' rhetoric and his presidency enshrined the gadfly's credo as national policy."

Tax Cutter in the White House

As he had done when Ronald Reagan ran for governor, Howard Jarvis decided to hit the road to help Reagan in his quest for the presidency. Jarvis traveled around the country starting in New York City and working west, scheduling press conferences to support the Reagan run for the White House.

At the first stop in New York City, coffee was set up at the back of the room, donuts were piled high on a silver serving platter—and not one reporter showed up. It was more than a year since Proposition 13 had passed and the New York media apparently was not interested in what the California tax fighter had to say.

Jarvis was not particularly disappointed. He'd held many press conferences over the years that did not draw any attention. He learned from those experiences. To get attention for his cause, Jarvis used to schedule press conferences at the Los Angeles Press Club immediately after a press conference he was sure would bring out the media. He hoped he could convince some reporters to stay and talk about his concern. With the demise of the Los Angeles Press Club, those who have trouble getting their stories to the media today cannot copy this clever tactic.

The "Jarvis for Reagan" campaign moved on and interest in Jarvis increased—some. One reporter showed up for the press event in Pittsburgh—he got an exclusive interview. Then, press attendance doubled in Cleveland to two.

Jarvis was on a roll, and in fact, the number of reporters increased at every stop as he traveled west. The last event was in Portland, Oregon and the room was full of cameras and reporters. Part of that may have had to do with the property tax battle that was going on in Oregon at the time. A number of Oregon property tax initiatives were defeated before one passed years later.

In Indianapolis, Jarvis completed his press conference supporting Reagan, talking about the former governor's tax-cutting efforts in California and what he expected Reagan would bring to the White House. After the press conference, he stepped to a phone bank in the hotel lobby and called a young congressman running for the U.S. Senate in Indiana attempting to upset veteran Birch Bayh. Jarvis asked the congressman if he wanted Jarvis's endorsement

and Dan Quayle said, "Yes." A press release was issued by
the Quayle campaign but Jarvis already was on his way to
Kansas City.

An Indianapolis reporter called in Kansas City,
sounding a bit irritated, and asked why Jarvis had not
announced his endorsement of Quayle at the press
conference in Indianapolis so that this news item could
be added to the story he was writing about Jarvis.
"Because," I explained, "he didn't want to endorse
anyone who didn't want his endorsement. He had to
clear it with Quayle first."

On election night in 1980, Jarvis planned to be at the
Century Plaza Hotel in Los Angeles to take part in Reagan's
victory party. But he decided to accept the invitation of
Orange County Republicans to join their election night
activities first, about 50 miles south of Century City.

After saying his "hellos" and being announced to the
crowd, Jarvis and his party got into their car and headed
to Los Angeles. On the radio, they heard the early
concession speech of President Carter and the victory
speech of the new president-elect from the Century Plaza
Hotel. By the time they reached the ballroom of the Century
Plaza, it was nearly empty.

But still, Jarvis was jubilant about Reagan's victory.
The headline in the next Jarvis Taxpayer Association
newsletter, *Taxing Times*, roared: "Tax Cutter in White
House."

The story read in part: "President-elect Reagan is one
of us. He's no Johnny-Come-Lately to cutting taxes. As
Governor of California, he cut billions. As a private citizen
in 1978, he was a strong supporter of Proposition 13. As a
presidential nominee, he has called for tax cuts ..."

The tax-cutting revolution that started in California
was moving to Washington, D.C.

"Give the Petition to the Damn Republicans"

Ronald Reagan was determined to follow the California example with an across—the-board tax cut. His proposal was to trim the income tax by 30% over three years.

Jarvis had been concerned with income taxes, too, back in California. In June 1980, when Reagan was winning the California primary on his way to capturing the Republican presidential nomination, Jarvis's plan to cut the California income tax in half, Proposition 9, was defeated at the polls. Anger at the income tax was centered more on federal taxes, as Jarvis discovered. But his California proposition had raised the issue in another high-profile campaign, and he would continue the crusade by helping Reagan lower the federal income tax.

Jarvis went to Reagan's inauguration, and was among the thousands who watched an inauguration for the first time from the west end of the Capitol. Reagan was facing west, where the revolution, which swept him into office, began. Reagan mentioned taxes in his inaugural address. "Those who do work are denied a fair return for their labor by a tax system which penalizes successful achievement and keeps us from maintaining full productivity."

The trip to Washington for the swearing-in was a last minute decision for Jarvis who had just come off a difficult eight-day tour of Texas supporting the efforts of the group "Texas 13" to bring the initiative process to the state. "Texas 13" was run by the state's former attorney general, Waggoner Carr, who had participated in the Kennedy assassination investigation. An affable storyteller, Carr had set up the use of small planes owned by different supporters, which ferried Jarvis from city to city, campaign stop to campaign stop, all over Texas. On the last night, Jarvis joked to an appreciative audience in Austin, the State Capitol, with Governor Bill Clements in attendance: "I didn't realize Texas was so big, I've been flying for eight days and I can't get out of it." Texans like those "big" Texas jokes.

In Fort Worth, Jarvis was hosted by Eddie Chiles, an early supporter of Jarvis taking his tax crusade national. Chiles was owner of the Texas Rangers baseball club and would later bring into the ownership future president, George W. Bush. At the Fort Worth event, Jarvis was introduced to a well-off, genteel group by someone who had his doubts about the initiative process, or as he put it, "government by the masses."

Jarvis rocked the audience when he took the microphone and began, "I'd rather have government by the masses than government by the asses."

The Texas trip had been exhausting and Jarvis's last minute decision to fly across the country to the inaugural came with no preparation for the trip. Although reserved tickets were found for the swearing-in ceremony, no tickets were available for the top priority California Inaugural Ball where the new president would spend the most time. Jarvis ended up at the Tennessee-Iowa-Arizona Ball sitting with an Arizona American Indian leader in his special box enjoying the evening as the Indian chief and the chief tax cutter received visitors.

Reagan immediately set to work on his tax cut plan, and Jarvis tried to rally support from around the country.

Following the victory of Proposition 13, Jarvis decided to set up new taxpayer organizations, one to work in California to protect Proposition 13, the California Tax Reduction Movement, now called the Howard Jarvis Taxpayers Association, and one to deal with national tax issues, as well as to assist taxpayer groups in other states called the American Tax Reduction Movement (ATRM). Jarvis aired a national television broadcast to attract members to ATRM. The United Organizations of Taxpayers still was in existence and Jarvis still was in charge, but it was a volunteer organization and Jarvis felt he needed a full-time organization to deal with the attacks he could see forming against Proposition 13.

It was the American Tax Reduction Movement with Jarvis at the head that spearheaded the effort to support the Reagan tax cuts. Sending thousands upon thousands of letters and enclosed petitions around the country, over a matter of months, Jarvis amassed a phenomenal 672,000 petitions containing about 2 million signatures supporting the tax cut.

Jarvis would deliver those petitions in person to Congress. His organization arranged to ship the 2 ½ tons of petitions to Washington where they were set up in a room in the capitol basement for the purposes of a press conference. Boxes were not only piled up behind Jarvis but a wall of boxes was set up in front of him and used as a podium for the media's microphones. As impressive as the number of boxes were, it was made to look more so for the television cameras by placing a number of boxes on a table in the back, then hiding the table with more boxes in front to cover up the table.

A room full of journalists recorded Jarvis's support for the Reagan tax cuts. Then, as the journalists had been advised beforehand, Jarvis took one symbolic petition and headed upstairs to the chamber of the Speaker of the House to present it to Speaker Tip O'Neill. He wanted to show the Speaker, leader of the opposition Democrats, the widespread national support for the Reagan tax cut plan.

The Speaker's office had been informed ahead of time that Jarvis would be delivering the petition with media in tow. In fact, Jarvis had run into O'Neill when walking the capitol halls the day before and they had a friendly chat, Jarvis telling him he would be by the next day with a petition representing all the petitions he was bringing to Washington in support of the tax cut.

But, when Jarvis showed up at the speaker's office with his petition, O'Neill was not amused. He had just finished his scheduled briefing with reporters and was leaving his office when Jarvis tried to hand him the petition. O'Neill refused to take it, brusquely moving past Jarvis like a big lineman clearing the way for a running back, and muttered to Jarvis, "Give the petition to the damn Republicans."

This little bit of show biz served Jarvis well. There had been no coordination with the White House about Jarvis's supportive effort on behalf of the president, nor about his media event in the capitol. Back in the hotel, we made some calls to the White House to inform them what had been done. Soon, a call came back inviting Jarvis to the White House for a meeting with the president.

President Reagan's Assistant for Public Liaison, Elizabeth Dole, now U.S. Senator from North Carolina, escorted Jarvis into the Oval Office. An official White House photo of the president greeting his old California comrade showed the two men in a warm handshake, wide smiles crossing their faces. In his hand, Jarvis held rolled up sheets of paper. They were political cartoons Jarvis had conceived and had a cartoonist draw up which he wanted to share with the president. One cartoon poked fun at Jerry Brown's current difficulties dealing with a med-fly infestation in California. The meeting lasted 15 minutes with the President thanking Jarvis for his support on the tax cuts. They discussed some tax cut strategy and did a little California reminiscing before Jarvis left.

On this trip to Washington, and on other trips to the city, Jarvis would meet regularly with Congressman Jack Kemp who had been fighting for tax cuts even before Ronald Reagan was elected. Kemp was a strong believer in the message of Proposition 13, and he and Jarvis talked about spreading the message of tax cuts, economic freedom, and economic growth across the nation. They also talked politics. With Reagan just recently elected, Kemp already was looking down the road, trying to figure how he could "get hold of the (Republican) convention" in 1988 for a presidential bid.

The tax cuts passed Congress, although at 25% across the board, they were slightly smaller than the president had sought originally, but Congress had made other tax-cutting concessions.

Kemp believed the tax cuts were a direct result of Proposition 13. He said, at the time of Prop 13's 20th anniversary, "There is no doubt that Prop 13 and its passage in 1978 led to the Reagan tax cuts . . . also led, in my opinion, to Margaret Thatcher adopting tax cuts in the U. K. It was the most important popular, small 'd' democratic, grass-roots referendum movement where people said 'enough.'"

When the federal tax cut was approved, Jarvis said on a radio commentary, "The tax battle is over. But the war will continue. The war will be between those who push the interests of a party like the Speaker, and those who push the interests of the country, like the President. I know which side I'm on."

In his newspaper column syndicated to about a dozen papers around the country, Jarvis wrote, "Franklin Roosevelt told the world America will be the arsenal of democracy. I believe, in the years ahead, we will be the arsenal of liberty for all Americans, and Reaganomics can help us get there."

"The Buttons Nearly Popped off My Vest"

Ronald Reagan did not forget that Proposition 13 helped him achieve his decades-long goal of cutting federal taxes. While he often talked about his Reagan Revolution coming from the west like a prairie fire, he said the match that started the fire was Proposition 13.

On one occasion, Howard Jarvis attended a luncheon speech given by President Reagan in Los Angeles. When Jarvis returned to the office and I asked him how the speech went, he said, "When the president said, 'What we're trying to do in Washington is in the spirit of Proposition 13,' the buttons nearly popped off my vest."

When Proposition 13 reached its fifth anniversary, President Reagan wrote from the White House on May 24, 1983:

> Dear Howard,
>
> I am proud to send my greetings and congratulations to you and those gathered to celebrate the Fifth Anniversary of Proposition 13.
>
> Proposition 13 brought welcome relief to property owners who were stifled with excessively high tax rates, and remains a household word in our country. Largely because of your efforts, the people of California sent that message to Sacramento—enough is enough!
>
> The California tradition of trend-setting continues and I believe Proposition 13 contributed a good deal to the grass-roots demand for tax relief nationwide. In spite of the opposition and all the false charges, we've given the people a tax cut that is fair and equitable across the board. We are going to keep fighting to stem the tide of government growth and bring more tax relief to the American people. The philosophy is simple but sound: The people are better qualified to spend their own money than government.
>
> Nancy and I join our fellow Californians and citizens all across the land in this salute to you.

The First Winner of the Howard Jarvis Tax Fighter Award

On May 16, 1992, former President Ronald Reagan attended a meeting of the Howard Jarvis Taxpayers Association at a Los Angeles airport hotel ballroom to receive the first Howard Jarvis Tax Fighter Award.

Reagan said, "I am doubly honored to be here today, first, to receive this award in the name of Howard Jarvis, an old and dear friend, and second, to be recognized as a lifetime tax fighter in a nation that was founded on a tax revolt."

The award was a bronze bust of Howard Jarvis, glasses pushed down his nose as he looked over the glasses into the distance. The bust was heavy, and as I commented to the president, it was shatterproof. This elicited a smile from Reagan. A few weeks earlier, Reagan had been at a convention where he was presented a glass award, which had been shattered by a protestor who stormed the stage but did not hurt the president.

Because of the bust's weight, I never handed it to Reagan but whispered again that it was heavy and that maybe I should put it on the table and allow him to make his remarks. He finally agreed. But I got a gentle reminder after the ceremony that I should have handed him the award. In a picture-taking ceremony in a back room, the president told me he still worked around his ranch and he could handle the bust easily enough.

Reagan was effusive about Proposition 13 on this day. "With Proposition 13, we told government that since the power to tax is the essence of government, we citizens are going to take control of taxation."

He reminded the audience of about a thousand people that his own California tax reform package, Proposition 1, had been defeated, but said, "We tax reformers bear our scars proudly."

Reagan talked about how the American Revolution reversed the course of history with three little words: We the People. "We, the people, tell the government what to do, it doesn't tell us. This was a concept that was cherished by Howard Jarvis."

Reagan continued, "The spirit of Proposition 13 will go on because it is an extension of the beliefs on which this country was built. Joel, as you once said, 'How we agree to tax ourselves is a measure of our freedom,' and that's right."

In his speech, the president tied both the taxpayer revolution and the Reagan Revolution to their inspirational and spiritual source—the American Revolution.

PART SIX

Defending the Tax Revolt

A Battle of Words

In David Hackett Fischer's exciting re-telling of the opening battles of the American Revolution in his book, *Paul Revere's Ride*, he argues that there was a second battle of Lexington and Concord. The first battle occurred on the battlefield, in which the British and Americans fired the first shots of the war in Lexington, with the British pushing the Americans from the village green and the Americans pushing back at Concord Bridge, and then harassing the British soldiers' retreat all the way back to Boston.

The second battle was one of propaganda—a battle of words—for the hearts and minds of American citizens in the New World and British citizens in the old. Was the fighting at Lexington and Concord necessary for a people desiring freedom, or were they the acts of uncivilized frontiersmen attempting to disrupt the proper order? Were the grievances sufficient to break the colonies from the Mother Country? American leaders thought so and they later detailed those grievances in the Declaration of Independence. But the propaganda war also had to succeed in the colonies and in England outside of the elite who conducted the war. Eventually, it did.

And, so Fischer concluded, " . . . the fighting on April 19 was a minor reverse for British arms, and a small success for the New England militia. But the ensuing contest for popular opinion was an epic disaster for the British government, and a triumph for American Whigs."

Proposition 13 won on the battlefield. After a hard-fought campaign, Proposition 13 was a clear winner with voters. However, the second battle of Proposition 13 still rages for the hearts and minds of the average Californian, and the people who look at California from afar.

Those who oppose Proposition 13 have large and expensive megaphones from which to make their arguments. The measure is constantly blamed in the media, especially the editorial pages of newspapers, for ills that plague California. Out-of-state media often follow the lead of their local brethren or take the message from the governing class that Proposition 13 was bad and has hurt California's schools, building of infrastructure, and government's flexibility to serve the people well. Academics, especially those who toil in the public institutions and are subsidized by the taxpayers, also have been harsh on Proposition 13.

Most of all, government chafes under the limits that Proposition13 put in place. When government fails at a task, or takes too long to respond, often it is declared to be Proposition 13's fault. Some people in government now believe they have a ready excuse for failure.

Despite the constant anti-13 drumbeat, the people still support the measure. They know it has offered them taxpayer protections. People outside of California who generally only hear negative stories about Proposition 13 may not have a good image of what it has done for the people. However, even if you hear the negative stories and you live in California, you know how you're protected by Proposition 13's limits on government and your right to vote on taxes.

As the years stretch away from the time of the successful revolution, new actions and activities related to Proposition 13 have occurred. There have been attempts to weaken the tax revolt, and efforts to strengthen it. Just because Proposition 13 was overwhelmingly successful at the polls did not mean that those who want bigger government and more tax revenue gave up the fight.

Ross Johnson, elected to the California Assembly for the first time as one of the "Proposition 13 babies" said, "Prop 13 and Howard Jarvis were on the forefront of the mood for change to reduce taxes and the size of government. However, when I got up to the Legislature, it quickly became obvious to me we were like a boxer in a ring with a wily veteran. We made a lucky punch and knocked him down but he got up and the battle was not over."

In fact, the battle raged on.

Prop 9

Howard Jarvis's first attempt to make the tax revolt broader was Proposition 9 in 1980, a plan to cut the state income tax in half. As already mentioned, people disliked the federal income tax with almost the same passion that they disliked the property tax, but California's state income tax, even though it was one of the highest in the nation, was not put in the same category as either the property tax or the federal income tax.

However, Proposition 9 received plenty of attention from the media as Jarvis picked up his crusade for the taxpayers again. The measure was on the June 1980 primary ballot.

The campaign started well. In one of his first appearances for Proposition 9 at the Channel City Club in Santa Barbara on April 1, 60 pickets protesting the new proposed tax cut greeted Jarvis. Inside the meeting, Jarvis opened his speech by saying, "Public employees must have a holiday today and they're all outside." The capacity crowd of 600 applauded. Jarvis could feel a revival of the Proposition 13 spirit.

Initially, the chief debater the opposition put up against Jarvis was former Judge Bruce Sumner, a leading Orange

County Democrat, who had filed a suit trying to throw Proposition 13 off the ballot. Jarvis quickly disposed of Sumner by claiming he was getting fat off the taxpayers and listed all the pensions he would receive from serving in a myriad of public offices. There were four, as I recall. No more Sumner. The "NO" campaign eventually settled on Mickey Kantor, a Los Angeles lawyer who went on to become President Clinton's Commerce Secretary, and Ira Reiner, a Democrat who had supported Proposition 13 and would later serve as Los Angeles County District Attorney, as their main spokesmen.

The "NO" campaign again dealt with potential cuts in services, but this time added the argument that tax savings would go to the rich. The universities made an extraordinary effort to get involved in the politics of Proposition 9 with the president of the University of California system suggesting that fees would increase and the Psychology Department of San Jose State sending out acceptance letters to its Master's program "contingent on the failure of Proposition 9." The president of San Jose State eventually rebuked the department for the letters.

Polls indicated that the voters started to turn against the measure and Jarvis tried harder to get his message out. He was over-scheduled. One day, Jarvis had a Los Angeles appearance in the morning, a San Diego appearance mid-morning, an L. A. campaign stop at noon and then back to San Diego for the afternoon and a 6 p.m. live television appearance. After all that came a helicopter ride on the station's chopper to San Diego's Lindbergh Field, where the commercial plane to Los Angeles was held a few minutes for his arrival and back he went to Los Angeles for an evening speech.

The exhausting schedule and constant bombardment from the opposition took its toll. A tired Jarvis attacked his opponents and the press went overboard in castigating him. In a May 4 editorial in the *Los Angeles Times* titled "The

Cannon is Loose!", Jarvis was compared to a loose cannon on a "recent rampage" through San Luis Obispo County. The editorial noted Jarvis referred to county government as dumb and crooked.

What Jarvis was referring to was a situation years before when he was trying to help a homeowner with a property tax problem and had run into resistance from county officials who either didn't know where certain information was, or tried to stonewall him.

Still, the *Times* editorial decided to go into the gutter by quoting a third party: "The most charitable explanation of the (Jarvis) performance was offered by one county official who said the cannon was probably loaded."

The *Los Angeles Herald Examiner* declared that during the Proposition 9 campaign, Howard Jarvis had one big enemy and one big ally. His enemy, they said, was himself, "He's master of colossal overstatement and blowhard hyperbole, but that's Howard Jarvis." The paper admitted that Jarvis's ally was the political establishment, which gave him fodder to attack.

But Jarvis was also the victim of uncontrolled hostility, which led to the most bizarre incident of the campaign. Jarvis had accepted an invitation to speak at California State University, Sacramento. The invitation came from a journalism student who would ask Jarvis questions before an audience sitting in folding chairs in an outdoor quad area where students and faculty or anyone else could stop and listen.

The area filled up quickly, and the young moderator soon lost control of his program. He wanted to start off with a segment about Jarvis, the man, a bit of history. The audience was not interested. They hooted down the questions and wanted to get into the meat of a discussion on Proposition 9 and Proposition 13, as well.

The questions were generally hostile. Jarvis responded in kind and things heated up. Jarvis broke off the event a few minutes before it was scheduled to end. With a police escort, we were moved toward our car that was parked at the edge of the quad. Students, faculty and outsiders swarmed around screaming and yelling. Cameras caught the whole event.

One woman, described by a newspaper as a former Davis, California community activist, yelled to Jarvis that he ought to go back to Utah. Jarvis responded, "Why don't you go to Nevada? In a house they have over there, you couldn't make a quarter."

When we got into the car, students surrounded the car and continued to yell, a few pounded on the hood and trunk. After a few tense moments, campus police were finally able to clear a path and we drove away.

Later, the woman sued Jarvis for slander. The trial took place five years later. Jarvis didn't recall making the remark and told that to his attorney, Trevor Grimm. However, tapes of the incident recorded Jarvis making the remark in the wild melee. Grimm told Jarvis he had stipulated that, basically, Jarvis said what he said, and the defense would be on different grounds.

When the trial started, the lawyers for the woman played a tape of the incident they had received from television news cameras covering the event. Chairs were set up in front of the jury box for Jarvis, Grimm and me, with Jarvis on my left and Grimm on my right, our backs to the jury so we could all watch the tape at the same time.

On the screen, as Jarvis moved toward the car, screaming coming from all around, Jarvis could be heard saying, "Why don't you go to Nevada? In a house they have over there, you couldn't make a quarter."

And, in the silence of the courtroom, Jarvis muttered loud enough for us to hear: "I didn't say that!"

Grimm pounded me on my knee. Like I could do something about it. What had the jury thought? Jarvis said what he said on the tape, and here he was in the courtroom denying it. What they probably thought was they didn't hear what he said in the courtroom correctly. What else would explain it?

The trial went on and Jarvis won. The woman tried to portray herself as greatly affected by the incident—as a mild lady, a victim of circumstance so victimized that she occasionally crawled under tables to hide in a fetal position. But, Grimm had secured a newspaper picture of her taken at the event and had it blown up to four feet by three feet. He pinned it to a rolling blackboard and placed it in front of the jury. It showed an angry woman, mouth open, fists clenched, who appeared to be screaming at the top of her lungs. Foolishly, her attorneys left the picture in front of the jury when they conducted their questioning. The jury returned with their verdict in a very short time.

And, speaking of quarters, Jarvis debated Proposition 9 with San Francisco Mayor Dianne Feinstein on a San Francisco television station. He bet her a quarter Proposition 9 would pass and she took the bet. Partly because of the recent success of California's property tax cut and talk of federal income tax cuts in the Reagan campaign, the voters were in no mood to cut the state income tax. Proposition 9 failed. Jarvis paid off his bet by sending Feinstein a quarter encased in plastic and mounted on a wood block with a nice inscription on an attached plaque.

Feinstein responded with a thank-you note, "Dear Howard, I was delighted to receive your quarter ... typically, however, you wouldn't let me spend it."

Con Job

Howard Jarvis and his taxpayers' association were not down for long. He sponsored Proposition 7 on the June 1982 ballot to index the state income tax for inflation.

Without indexing, which adjusts tax brackets for inflation, a mere raise to keep workers' salaries up with inflation could throw those workers into a higher tax bracket, and despite the raise, taxpayers actually would lose money. Although he was ill for much of the campaign, Jarvis led Proposition 7 to a landslide victory.

He explained on his *Byline* radio commentary, "Politicians say they hate inflation. They don't. They love it because it brings more and more money to government, and they don't even have to pass a tax bill to get it. It's the citizens who hate inflation. It destroys their income."

Even if politicians didn't get it, voters understood that their purchasing power was going down. A University of Southern California study had reported that real per-worker income had peaked in 1972. Now, it was hard enough keeping up with the costs of living, never mind paying government a premium on taxes.

By now, government bureaucrats were figuring out ways to get around Proposition 13's restrictions. A long battle of attrition had begun with government officials enlisting the dictionary in their war to get more from the taxpayers. By inventing new definitions for "revenue enhancements" such as: using century-old property assessment charges in innovative ways; creating new fees; or purposely misreading the language of Proposition 13, the bureaucrats' felt the restrictions placed on taxes by Proposition 13 could be circumvented.

The Howard Jarvis Taxpayers Association thought that practically all taxes were covered by its initiative. However, the courts were compliant with local governments in declaring that Proposition 13 did not cover many new revenue-raising devices.

Opponents claimed the measure was poorly written so they had to go to court. Of course, many times, government lawyers were simply on fishing expeditions hoping they would find a sympathetic judge to crack open a loophole in Proposition 13.

After the *Los Angeles Times* castigated Prop 13 as being bad law because "ten years later, the meaning of Proposition 13 still is being fought out in the courts," I responded with a letter published on January 9, 1989: "May I remind *The Times*, 200 years after adoption of the First Amendment to the U.S. Constitution guaranteeing freedom of the press, speech, and religion, it continues to face lawsuits clarifying exactly what it means."

Since the Legislature would take no action to deal with these end runs, Jarvis went back to the people. He qualified another initiative for the ballot (Proposition 36) to secure votes on new revenue raisers. KABC television and radio political commentator, Bruce Herschensohn, called Jarvis a "living legend."

"To prove that," he said, in one of his on-the-air commentaries, "look at how the opponents of Proposition 36 start their arguments against it. It's always with, 'I respect Howard Jarvis but ' . . .' and even in the Voter's Pamphlet, in the argument against 36, there's the phrase: 'despite Jarvis' good intentions.'

"In other words, the opposition to 36 is saying, 'Don't get me wrong. I'm not saying anything against him. It's the idea . . . '"

Herschensohn went on to say, "Suddenly, the words 'fees' and 'assessments' and any other word than can be thought of to skirt and get around 13 have been used because if they use the accurate word 'taxes', their jig is up."

The campaign was tough. A television ad pictured Howard Jarvis as a clown with a pipsqueak voice. Campaign literature declared that Paul Gann was opposing Prop 36, but a startled opposition saw their press conference disrupted by Gann entering the room and declaring he supported Proposition 36.

Speaker of the Assembly Willie Brown said after the election, "We put together the biggest con job we could and the people bought it."

But during the campaign, Jarvis fought back. He sent out letters showing how much taxes would go up if Proposition 36 were defeated. The envelopes said, "Property Tax Statement Enclosed." The opposition claimed the envelopes looked official and the press piled on.

In one memorable situation, the attempt to make hay with the envelope backfired. Jay Curtis, a member of the business-oriented California Taxpayers Association, who, in later years, would become a strong ally of the Jarvis organization, debated Jarvis on television one day and tried to make an issue out of the mailing. He pulled three or four envelopes from his pocket and charged that they were not official documents.

Jarvis responded, "We never said they were, but we send them to all property owners and with so many envelopes, you must own a lot of property and be rich."

Curtis changed the subject.

A tax, by any other name, has thorns. But the people had not been stuck enough yet to howl, so Proposition 36 was defeated.

"Howard Lives"

More negative court decisions came, and the right to vote on taxes was slipping away. Perhaps, the most important court case to go against Proposition 13 was the *City and County of San Francisco vs. Farrell* (1982). It was important not because the judges read the act differently than what the author intended, but because it went against one of the underlying principles that made up the core of Proposition 13—that the people control their government with the right to vote on taxes.

In the early years after the adoption of the initiative process in California, attempts were made by the political establishment to make it more difficult to use the initiative to alter the tax system. This effort came about after followers of Henry George, one of California's first original thinkers, tried to get his single-tax plan on the ballot six times but failed. To discourage future efforts to alter the tax system, opponents of the initiative process proposed nearly doubling the signatures needed to qualify a tax-related ballot measure.

The main sponsors of California's initiative system, including Governor Hiram Johnson and Dr. John Randolph Haynes, opposed this effort. They created a group called the League to Protect the Initiative, and in the group's literature it said, "The power to tax is the essence of government. The control of taxation is the control of government."

A Jarvis corollary would add: And we the people must control the government, therefore, we the people must control taxation. That is the spirit of Proposition 13 and that is why the *Farrell* decision had to be overturned.

The specific issue involved in the court case was that term "special taxes." Proposition 13 gave the people the right to vote on "special taxes" proposed by their local governments. The court determined that special taxes are levied for a specific purpose, say, raising taxes to be spent specifically on police. To the court, and to officials in San Francisco, that meant that taxes raised for general governmental purposes to be placed in the general fund needed no vote at all. That's not what Jarvis intended.

This issue, along with the end runs on taxes through the use of terms likes "fees" and "assessments," would cause the Howard Jarvis Taxpayers Association to go back to the voters a number of times to get back the right to vote on taxes.

Howard Jarvis, himself, made one last run at securing the right to vote on taxes. The measure he put forth was Proposition 62. The proposal, chiefly intended to overturn the *Farrell* decision, was on the November 1986 ballot and it passed. Because it was a statute and not a constitutional amendment, it, too, would be tied up in the courts for years, and made largely ineffective.

However, Howard Jarvis never got to vote on it. He died on August 12, 1986, a little more than one month before his 83rd birthday.

Many mourned for him, particularly the folks he directly helped by giving them the opportunity to battle a seemingly uncaring government and allowing them to keep their homes. But, as is the way of things, it is the dignitaries who usually leave a record behind, and many sent letters of regret that have been preserved.

President Ronald Reagan wrote, "Millions of Americans owe a large debt of gratitude to this man who was fiercely dedicated to his principles. Howard believed in this country and loved it with all his heart. I shall always cherish the memory of his loyalty."

United States Senator Pete Wilson wrote, "It was Howard who recognized earlier than most the flagrant wrong of government taking too much out of the pockets of the citizenry."

At a memorial service for Jarvis, Bruce Herschensohn read from a letter he received about Jarvis from former president Richard Nixon. "Like all pioneers, he was brash, iconoclastic, gutsy and tough. But the real reason for his success is the clarity of his cause and his tireless personal dedication to it. America has lost one of its most colorful and original public figures, and the California taxpayer, his greatest friend and advocate."

But Jarvis's friend, colleague and counsel Trevor Grimm may have said it best: "Howard's death was just a rumor."

"If your definition (of who Howard is) includes Howard's spirit ('never quit'), Howard's philosophy ('government must be limited'), Howard's goal ('government must do a day's work for a day's pay'), then every time that you get mad enough to do something about governmental expansion, abuse or sloth, and every time you follow through and actually do something about it, even though all the troops are arrayed against you, neither asking for nor giving quarter, then Howard lives."

HJTA

After Babe Ruth left the Yankees, they kept on winning. With Howard Jarvis gone, the Howard Jarvis Taxpayers Association (HJTA) moved ahead with its mission to protect the taxpayers. I became president after serving a total of seven years as an aide to Jarvis and as the organization's executive director. Noted economist Arthur Laffer served as chairman of the Board of Directors for about one year. Mrs. Estelle Jarvis remained on the Board and was joined by her sister, Dolores Tuttle, among others.

There was a need to keep up the fight against a full-time legislature. Some claim that it is not a legitimate, grass roots taxpayers' movement if paid advocates are working with the taxpayers. But, government officials trying to get tax dollars are paid, and organizations and businesses employee paid lobbyists. While taxpayers are out earning a living, they need to have full-time paid representation for their cause, too.

As Senator Ross Johnson said, after criticizing those who believed grass roots efforts like Proposition 13 are part of an initiative industry, "Government is the damn industry. Lobbyists for government, all city, county and agencies, people on government payrolls, they lobby other governments to spend more tax money. The taxpayers are underrepresented at these hearings."

The Howard Jarvis Taxpayers Association has been a full-time taxpayers' representative over the years against all kinds of attacks on taxpayers' wallets, both straightforward and disguised. Like the time Senator Henry Mello figured he discovered a way to extract more property taxes from homeowners with an "excise" tax on property "for the privilege of using or occupying that property for urban purposes." Don't try to analyze what that means. The simple translation was, "We want more of your tax money based on your property ownership." The money was supposed to be used for establishing an open-space authority in Santa Clara County, but HJTA saw the seeds of an ever-expanding use for a property "excise" tax. It would become a supplemental property tax.

HJTA informed its members of the bill and supplied postcards to mail to Governor George Deukmejian asking for his veto. Deukmejian's office reported that it received 52,000 postcards and additional phone calls opposed to the bill. The governor vetoed it. He wrote in his veto message, "This bill is clearly in violation of the letter and spirit of Proposition 13."

HJTA has kept in contact with its members mostly by mail. There is a clear comparison with the organization's outreach to its members and the famous Committee of Correspondence set up during the American Revolution. Letters kept members of the Committee of Correspondence up to date on the news of British activities. As one magazine article noted, the Committee had significant effect in arousing sentiment against arbitrary British taxation and administration. HJTA kept its members informed about action on the tax front that the daily newspapers did not cover. Members financially supported keeping the organization going because they knew that the victory of Proposition 13 would not end government's efforts to get into their pockets. As Howard Jarvis once put it, referring to the need to keep the organization financially viable: "A ship can't sail on yesterday's wind."

However, our mail didn't always get the expected

response. One day in the early 1980s, I received a phone call from an elderly lady who got one of our mailings and asked what it was all about. I explained the measure we were supporting and when finished, told her I hoped she agreed with us and would vote that way come election day.

She responded, "Oh, I agree with you all right, Mr. Fox. But I haven't voted since Roosevelt."

I did not ask which one.

The Association's strength in numbers peaked at over 300,000 but it has always maintained a strong core of taxpayer support from the average citizens needing someone to stand up for them. And it wasn't only the ordinary person who would support HJTA or call on HJTA for help, or to point out some tax administration malfeasance. It was not unusual for Jarvis to receive calls from Cary Grant or Ray Bradbury. HJTA membership rolls included the likes of movie actor Francis Lederer. Supporters have included film box-office star Arnold Schwarzenegger. Old-time baseball great Babe Herman sought out Jarvis after a speech in Glendale.

It is difficult to determine exactly how much the work of Howard Jarvis and HJTA has saved the California taxpayer. Estimates have been made that if Proposition 13 had not passed, taxpayers would have forked over hundreds of billions more to state and local government. Indexing the income tax was estimated to save an additional $100 billion. Successful lawsuits and the right to vote allowing taxpayers to turn down tax increases add billions more. There was one stretch in 1998 that HJTA lawsuits saved $4 billion alone. Then there was the effort of the American Tax Reduction Movement helping to pass the Reagan tax cuts. Members of HJTA were rewarded for their support.

The *Washington Post* said, "The Howard Jarvis Taxpayers Association in Los Angeles (is) a sort of national shrine to the modern anti-tax movement."

Proposition 13 and HJTA constantly are tested, not only by government power, but also by the power of nature. California is earthquake country and it had a couple of whoppers since Proposition 13 passed, not counting the metaphorical earthquake of Proposition 13 itself.

The 1989 Loma Prieta earthquake in northern California, which knocked out sections of the Bay Bridge and collapsed parts of the Nimitz Freeway on the East Bay, brought calls for tax increases to help pay for the damage. But, more to the point, it also gave opponents of Proposition 13 an opportunity to blast the initiative.

Pulitzer Prize–winning, *Los Angeles Times* editorial cartoonist Paul Conrad showed a car crushed by the freeway, and the license plate on the car read: Prop 13. On the same editorial page, Lenny Goldberg, long-time leader of the California Tax Reform Association, which is backed by public and private labor unions and advocates for tax increases, had an article criticizing Proposition 13, arguing that the collapse of the freeway was somehow tied to the ideological struggle over taxes.

The HJTA response, printed in the October 28, 1989 "Letters" section of the *Times*, castigated Conrad's approach and said this about Goldberg's argument:

> Lenny Goldberg makes the ridiculous statement that whereas a freeway collapse in New York would result from a contracting scandal, a collapse in California would be the result of an ideological scandal over taxes. Goldberg is trying to explain away the fact that disasters happen in high tax states without a Proposition 13. Such disasters are the Achilles' heel of his argument that high taxes would prevent the calamities. The collapse of the relatively newer overpasses in the Sylmar earthquake of 1971 occurred seven years before we had Proposition 13 during a high tax period in California.

In Goldberg's many debates over the years about taxes, and Proposition 13 in particular, he always strongly advocated his position but he had to admit that at times it was difficult. He often repeated the story of reading from the prayer book during the Passover Holiday about the Pharaoh sending his tax chiefs down upon the Hebrews, and his guests around the table would look up at him and ask, "Whose side are you on?"

The national media got into the debate about how Proposition 13 might have played a role in the effects of the earthquake when Ted Koppel asked on his October 18, 1989 *Nightline* show: "We all remember a few years ago, Proposition 13 rolled back taxes. That's fine, but that means there are going to be fewer funds available for necessary projects. Any instances where the money would have made a difference?"

To which the *Wall Street Journal* countered on October 24, "California's roads and bridges aren't funded by property taxes but by state and federal gasoline taxes. Both have been raised at least 30% in recent years, even while the price of gasoline has fallen. Dragging Prop. 13 into this story is a pretty long stretch."

Taxes were raised to deal with the effects of the Loma Prieta earthquake, but when a second major earthquake hit the Northridge area in southern California's San Fernando Valley in 1994, taxes were not the answer. It is true some politicians called for a tax increase, but in a January 31, 1994, *Los Angeles Times* opinion piece, HJTA argued against them.

We were in the middle of a debilitating recession and taxes would hurt hopes of recovery. Besides, in the five years since the Loma Prieta earthquake, the state sales tax had increased 1 ¼ cents and tax on gasoline had doubled. We recommended taking the federal aid package offered by the Clinton White House. Some Republicans were balking but our answer was: "Even John Wayne Republicans cheer when the cavalry rides to the rescue of the besieged wagon train."

Tax policy would seem to be a real dry business, but it can be entertaining. Some even write jokes about it—but in Los Angeles, they would probably be taxed.

The Los Angeles City Council raised a hullabaloo over taxing writers who worked in their homes. Writing is a business, said the bureaucrats, and businesses must pay a business tax.

Having to pay taxes on their home businesses, the writers probably felt like their fellow writer, Henry David Thoreau, who recorded in his diary, September 8, 1859: "I went to the store the other day to buy a bolt for our front door, for as I told the storekeeper, the governor was coming here. 'Aye,' said he, 'and the legislature, too.' Then I will take two bolts, said I."

Eventually, the writers worked a compromise on the tax, but it didn't stop the entertainment. The material is plentiful. Consider what you can discover from a newspaper in just one day. The *Los Angeles Daily News* on September 14, 1995 was quite entertaining, or perhaps sobering, for those concerned with their tax dollars.

First, there was the story of the $60 million Los Angeles bond issue to refit a half-dozen city buildings with fire sprinkler systems. The city took the money, refit one building with new sprinklers and put some new sprinklers in a couple of other structures. Then the city used the rest of the funds to purchase a building for the personnel department at a cost more than the building was worth, then declared it was out of money to finish the sprinkler installation job.

Reading deeper into the same edition of the paper, we learned that the state Attorney General's Office was looking into why, after 10 years and $1.4 million tax dollars, the promised Hollywood show-business museum had not been built.

We turned a few more pages and discovered that City Hall seismic retrofitting would cost 66% more than the original estimate of $150 million. But not to worry, some city officials said, they could find the additional money in a seismic safety bond measure.

Why does that particular bond issue have a familiar ring? Turn back to the first story on the sprinkler bond and you read that different city officials believed they could make up the needed money to finish the sprinkler job using funds from that same seismic safety retrofitting bond!

Bad estimates, interchangeable bonds, money that seemed to disappear, too much money spent on a purchase that wasn't supposed to be made in the first place—who needed an entertainment museum in Hollywood when you could get all the perverse entertainment you wanted by reading about City Hall in action?

Despite these types of shenanigans, it is often HJTA that must fight for respect. Disrespect comes readily in the arena of bitter philosophical debate. When the League of Women Voters, sponsors of the 1988 presidential debates between George H. W. Bush and Michael Dukakis, got into an argument over the debate format and resigned from sponsoring the final debate, a presidential debate commission solicited funds to put on the debate. It was to be held in the Pauley Pavilion basketball arena on the campus of UCLA.

Howard Jarvis had created a Taxpayer Foundation when he set up his tax-fighting group. The Foundation did not deal in politics but rather gave scholarships and software to universities and funded reports and books on economics and taxes. The foundation decided to come to the aid of the debate commission and made a large contribution to the cause. As a thank you, the commission said it would note the Jarvis Foundation contribution in the official program, and that the top five contributors would be thanked publicly before the invitation-only crowd and media attending the event.

When the time came for the thank you, the national

chairmen of the Republican and Democratic parties took the stage. Democratic Chairman Paul Kirk had the job of thanking the five big donors. He thanked four. He didn't forget the *Los Angeles Times* or Arco. He did forget to mention the largest donor: The Howard Jarvis Taxpayers Foundation. I wonder why.

Ridicule is part of disrespect, and sometimes, we bring it on ourselves. San Diego was considering passing bonds for a new baseball park downtown. We were asked to oppose the project and agreed, signing the ballot argument for the "NO" side. A reporter called and asked if I read all the material about the sports stadium. I said, "No" but I had read enough to know it was a taxpayer rip-off.

The article portrayed me as a fool who made a knee-jerk reaction. An executive of the local taxpayer's group, one associated with business interests who supported the stadium, called to criticize.

It was not handled well, I admit. But there was vindication of sorts. The bonds passed, the costs were outrageous, and a scandal followed. You don't have to read it all to recognize a taxpayer rip-off.

Speaking of sports stadiums, in Los Angeles officials were trying to build a football stadium using taxpayers' money and running into severe and, ultimately, successful resistance. National Football League Commissioner Paul Tagliabue said, "We all understand the reality of taxes in California since someone named Jarvis came on the national scene."

But then, when you least expect it, respect may come from a truly surprising source. As mentioned more than once, our tax-cutting efforts were not warmly received by the *Los Angeles Times*—except for this one time. HJTA had threatened a lawsuit against Los Angeles County for a pension-spiking scheme in which money held out from county employee paychecks would be allocated to the last year of work in order to increase the salary from which the worker's pension was calculated. In some extreme cases, a county employee could get higher income in retirement than he or she got while working. When we went after this outrageous scheme, even the *Los Angeles Times* was on our side. The paper had editorialized against the county process. On the day we held a press conference in front of the Board of Supervisors offices, *The Times'* reporter covering the event said he was told by his editor that our story would run on the front page. Hard to believe.

But it didn't happen. It wasn't that the reporter was leading us on. It's just that later that day, the Simi Valley jury in the Rodney King cops' trial came back with their "not guilty" verdict and riots erupted in Los Angeles. We didn't make the front page.

Don't Blame Prop 13

The Berlin Wall had come down, Communism was dead, and suddenly, California was in trouble. It was the early 1990s, a time of celebration in the world. California suffered from a reverse spin on the so-called peace dividend. Compounding a national recession, California lost many important jobs connected to the defense industry. What became a rough financial ride in the rest of the country became the worst governmental fiscal hit in California since the Great Depression. When citizens' income is down, the taxes they pay to government are down. And when government doesn't have enough money to pay its bills, well, in California, according to government officials and many in the media, its all Prop 13's fault.

At a state capitol rally sponsored by the state teachers' union, Jesse Jackson proclaimed Proposition 13 "a scud missile which must be blown from the sky." The *Long Beach Press-Telegram* railed against the "accursed" Prop 13.

Cursed perhaps by the establishment, but not by the people. Florence Waldman of Chatsworth asked a sarcastic question in a letter to the *Los Angeles Daily News*: "Please tell me, is the fact that our whole country and the whole world are in recession the fault of Proposition 13?"

The Howard Jarvis Taxpayers Association felt it had to take a stand against the constant barrage of criticism against Proposition 13. HJTA wanted the legislators in Sacramento to know that the people still stood behind the tax-cutting initiative. During the peak of the fight over the budget deficit in June 1991, we purchased a weekday ad in the Capitol's largest newspaper, the *Sacramento Bee*.

In big red letters at the top of a page the ad read: DON'T BLAME PROPOSITION 13!

Below that the ad went on to say that attacks on Proposition 13 by many public officials and journalists had reached a "fever pitch." The ad refuted the notion that Prop 13 stalled government revenue increases with a list of facts on how much taxes had increased in the thirteen years since Proposition 13 passed, including the note that "California's public education budget is larger today than the entire state budget was when Proposition 13 passed."

Then the ad concluded: "Under no circumstances should Proposition 13 be altered or weakened as part of the budget process."

Mrs. Howard Jarvis and I signed the ad in large script. But below our signatures were the names that really counted. Under a message that read: "We the undersigned, Members of the Howard Jarvis Taxpayers Association, say to the State Legislature, 'Don't Blame Proposition 13,'" were the names of members who responded to our request to put their names on the ad and to help sponsor it. The names appeared in six-point type and were divided by counties. The names went on to the next page ... and the next page ... and the next page ... and the next page ... and the next page.

Five full pages of names in tiny six-point type plus the names below the text of the ad on the first page. A full six-page ad in all. About 50,000 names, if anyone bothered to count.

And at the bottom of the last page, appeared the coup de grace. It read simply: "Partial List" (which was true!).

Still, there was a budget deficit to deal with and new governor, Pete Wilson, was in the crosshairs. Wilson had served as a state assemblyman, mayor of San Diego, and United States senator, so he knew his way around politics when he became governor. Wilson had opposed Proposition 13 as mayor of San Diego, and as a candidate for the Republican nomination for governor the year Proposition 13 was on the ballot. That year, when a reporter said he heard Howard Jarvis was going to go fishing, Wilson broke into a smile and said jokingly, "I'd like to go find Howard Jarvis fishing—and drown him."

But, the truth is, Jarvis liked Wilson. In a debate with Wilson on Prop 13, Jarvis admitted, "If they had all run their cities like Pete Wilson has run San Diego, we wouldn't need Proposition 13."

To solve the problem of the massive budget deficit, larger in percentage terms to the overall budget than Ronald Reagan faced in his first year as governor, Wilson turned to a combination of spending cuts and the largest tax increase in California history—over $7 billion. Income taxes, sales taxes, vehicle license fees, and alcohol taxes were all increased.

Perhaps the most controversial part of the tax package, among many controversial parts, was a new tax on snack foods. It was difficult to determine exactly what a snack food was. Undoubtedly, candies were snacks. Were cookies snacks? Probably, said the taxing authorities. How about crackers? Well, we're not so sure about them.

To some, this particular tax increase became known as the "Ding Dong" tax because it taxed the chocolate-covered, hockey-puck-sized cake which carried that name. Such a delicious name for a tax increase. With the help of grocery merchants, the following year an initiative was placed on the ballot to repeal the snack tax and it passed overwhelmingly, facing hardly any opposition.

Another proposed tax was extending the sales tax to newspapers. This raised the concern of some in the publishing business—and confused some in the business of writing editorials.

In the *San Francisco Examiner's* lead editorial on February 11, 1991 titled "Raise State Taxes," the newspaper argued that taxes must be raised to close the budget deficit instead of making drastic cuts in programs for schools and the poor. The editorial listed a whole slew of taxes that could be raised, and included a recommendation saying, "Closing other loopholes identified by Sen. Wadie Deddah, D-Chula Vista, would raise another $385 million."

"We recommend this list to the governor and the legislature . . ." the editorial concluded.

That recommendation lasted three days.

On February 14, the newspaper sent a Valentine's Day present to itself in an editorial titled *On Taxes*, which appeared on the bottom of the editorial page. Following is the editorial in its entirety:

> Our editorial earlier this week urging higher taxes to close the state's budget deficit has engendered some misinterpretation, which we'd like to clear up.
>
> We did not endorse any specific measures, but we suggested that the governor and the Legislature "take a close look at" a variety of tax measures, including closing some tax loopholes. In this list, we mentioned a proposal by state Sen. Wadie Deddah, D-Chula Vista, that would raise $385 million by imposing a sales tax on candy, snack food, newspapers and other periodicals.
>
> As we have an inherent conflict of interest on the newspaper sales tax idea, we recuse ourselves and take no position on it.

Huh? It is okay to tax someone else but when the tax is on you, that's another matter. And, where is there any "conflict" if you suggest taxing yourself? Despite what the Valentine's Day editorial claimed, suggesting it only said "look at" these taxes, the first editorial did, in fact, send a recommended list of taxes to the governor and legislature. Minds changed when they discovered one of the tax increases was on them.

An opinion piece I submitted to the *Los Angeles Times* appeared in the January 14, 1991 edition as follows:

> I have often been asked if there is any tax increase I would support readily. "Yes," I respond, "a tax on newspapers." . . . I attribute my reaction to a touch of bitterness, a common malady for those who toil in the public arena and whose ideas are trashed by the media . . . . Too many California newspapers, particularly editorial pages, have been hard on the tax revolt, blaming it for many ills in the state. My files are full of newspaper editorials calling for increased taxes. So, my reaction says, raise taxes on newspapers and let them see what we mean about tax increases hurting . . .
>
> Now, with Wilson's proposal on the table, my opportunity is at hand. The temptation to support the tax is magnified by the added reward of being able to boast that my organization is not always against tax increases (which we are not) and pull out an endorsement for the newspaper tax like an old soldier pulling out a war medal to relive past glory.
>
> But when the chips are on the table, I cannot play the cards. We should not raise taxes on newspapers.

The sales tax on newspapers and snack tax were part of the $7 billion tax package that passed. And, you know what happened? The tax increases prolonged California's recession. In fact, the bureaucrats' calculations on how much the new taxes would bring in were way off. The state got far less money than projected after the tax increases were put in place.

Wilson wrote an exclusive article to HJTA members for the *Taxing Times* newsletter defending his position on the tax increases. He said, "To raise taxes goes against my every instinct." He wrote about his long record as a fiscal conservative and argued that many changes were made in the budget negotiations that would lead to government efficiencies.

However, Wilson came to regret the tax increase in later years. He called it a "mistake."

Hard budgetary times beset California for the next couple of years. To deal with an on-going budget crisis, the governor and legislature decided to look elsewhere than tax increases. The idea was presented to shift some property tax money to schools, essentially ending the post-Proposition 13 decision to keep more property taxes with local government and take care of the loss of school property taxes with state funds. By requiring more property taxes to go to schools, the state was relieved of some of its school-funding obligation and it could use the freed-up funds as it wished.

Of course, this tax shift brought more accusations from local government that Proposition 13 was at fault by limiting property taxes in the first place.

Under the *Serrano* court decisions of the 1970s, basing school funding on property tax wealth was considered unequal protection of the laws. A similar tax rate on property in Beverly Hills and San Fernando would bring in much different revenue to fund education. To balance education funding, the state decided it had to lessen its school funding reliance on the property tax. So, moving to more state funding of schools was a way to satisfy the court's *Serrano* decrees. It should have remained that way, with property taxes staying with local government to pay for property-related services.

By shifting property taxes, big holes were left in local budgets. Local governments would look to fill those holes by searching for loopholes and end runs around Proposition 13.

PART SEVEN

Proposition 13 in the United States Supreme Court

"A Lawsuit Will be Filed in California within 30 Seconds"

Unlike an earthquake that hits unexpectedly but with full force, the first signs that Proposition 13 might be in a life-and-death struggle before the United States Supreme Court came softly. We heard something about a case from faraway West Virginia that was headed to the Supreme Court and that this case could somehow affect Proposition 13.

In December 1988, the justices listened to arguments in the West Virginia case which concerned different property tax assessments for similarly situated properties. To many, the West Virginia situation was a mirror image of how California taxed its property under Proposition 13.

It is often called the "welcome stranger" method of taxation in which a new owner pays more in taxes based on the current purchase price of land, but long-time owners pay less in taxes because their property had been assessed at much lower valuations and had not been changed even as the current market value increased.

Lawyers for a coal company that was paying 35 times more in taxes than its neighbors said they were denied equal protection of the law. If the Supreme Court agreed, there was a chance that Proposition 13 would face the same challenge.

Proposition 13 allowed for different taxes on neighboring properties depending on when the property was purchased. If someone owned a home since 1975 and saw taxes only go up 2% a year as Proposition 13 allowed, they would be paying much less than a neighbor who just purchased a house and had to pay taxes based on the purchase price.

The justices listening to the arguments on the West Virginia case were conscious that their ruling could affect Proposition 13. In fact, Justice William Brennan asked from the bench, "If the 'welcome stranger' method is a denial of equal protection, why isn't Proposition 13 equally invalid?"

No one knew what the justices' answer might be. Proposition 13 was unlike the West Virginia situation because Prop 13 was part of the state constitution. In West Virginia, the local assessor refused to recalculate the older assessments despite the law that it should be done.

HJTA had provided a friend of the court brief to warn the justices that any decision they made could affect Proposition 13. Jon Coupal, then an attorney with Pacific Legal Foundation, and now HJTA president, prepared the brief. After attending the hearing, I told the *Los Angeles Times*: "If they decide this is an equal protection violation, there will be a lawsuit filed in California within 30 seconds."

When the Supreme Court ruled on the case finding that the West Virginia assessor had violated the law, the court added a footnote that said the decision had no direct bearing on Proposition 13. However, the court seemed to be inviting a direct challenge to the California law.

It may have taken more than 30 seconds, but it was not long before three cases were filed declaring that Proposition 13's acquisition value formula was a violation of the equal protection provision of the United States Constitution.

The first test was filed by a Nevada corporation, Northwest Financial, Inc., doing business in California. Basing its claim on the West Virginia case, the company asked that its taxes be reduced on a home it purchased. In truth, had the court agreed that equal protection had been violated, taxes would have gone up, not down. To satisfy equal protection, it is likely that the state would have reverted to the old property tax system, resulting in a property tax increase across the state totaling over $8 billion.

The second challenge to Proposition 13's tax formula came in a lawsuit filed by R. H. Macy's department store. When Macy's Corporation reorganized, California law deemed the change in organization to be a change in ownership, allowing Macy's properties to be reassessed. A Macy's store in a northern California mall was assessed at a level much higher than similar Sears and J. C. Penney's stores in the same mall. Macy's complained that it was paying more per square foot than its competitors and that difference in taxes would have to be passed on to its customers through the price of its products. That tax difference meant there was unequal competition with the other large stores, a circumstance brought about because of Proposition 13. Thus, Macy's felt that not only was it a victim of unequal protection of the laws, but that its being forced to pay higher taxes than its competitor was an additional violation of the U.S. Constitution's Commerce Clause.

Perhaps because the executives of the Macy's firm were from another state, they did not understand the passion the people of California held for Proposition 13. The people did not take kindly to this assault on Prop 13, which could result in new taxes on everybody. Angry consumers cut up their Macy's credit cards and sent them back to the company. A political-type campaign began. Flyers were handed out and big political buttons were distributed with a red background and white letters declaring: BOYCOTT MACY'S.

The California business community also was upset with Macy's for filing the lawsuit. The concern was that if Macy's prevailed, the solution could be to raise taxes on all businesses, if not all property. Thus, the split-roll property tax system in which businesses and residences would be taxed on a different basis—something the business community tried so hard to avoid over the years—might become a reality due to a lawsuit by one of its own.

In June 1991, the United States Supreme Court agreed to hear the Macy's challenge to Proposition 13—and Macy's promptly withdrew it.

Macy's realized its public relations mistake and pulled the lawsuit in the face of the heated protest. A good thing, too, because while we always felt we could protect Proposition 13 before the Supreme Court on equal protection grounds, the commerce clause issue was a wild card, and we did not know how it might play out before the court.

The Northwestern Financial suit was not pursued and fell by the wayside. That left only a lawsuit by a Los Angeles lawyer who objected to paying more taxes than her neighbor on a modest home she had purchased. It was this case that made it all the way to the United States Supreme Court.

Life or Death for Proposition 13

Stephanie Nordlinger was an attorney who purchased a $170,000 home in the Baldwin Hills' section of Los Angeles in 1988. She found that she was paying five times more in property taxes than were her neighbors who lived in comparable homes since 1975. She filed suit on equal protection grounds using fellow public interest law attorneys who always objected to Proposition 13's tax limitations. Her chief attorney, Carlyle Hall, called Proposition 13's tax system an "outrageous" violation of equal protection of the law.

The lawyers were not the only ones who hoped Nordlinger would succeed. The *San Diego Union* noted on

December 17, 1990, "Such cases as that brought by the Baldwin Park (sic) woman have an eager rooting section in officials who have wanted, for 12 years, to be rid of Proposition 13 so they can return to the good old free taxing days."

Newly named Director of Legal Affairs for HJTA, Jon Coupal, participated in the state court hearings and argued that Proposition 13's acquisition value system not only had a "rational basis" but was, in fact, better than the current market value system in operation in other states. The case worked its way through the California court system with the courts dismissing it in deference to the California Supreme Court's *Amador* decision already declaring Proposition 13 to be constitutional. However, on October 7, 1991, the United States Supreme Court agreed to hear Nordlinger's appeal.

At a press conference held that afternoon, I said, "We will prove once and for all time that Proposition 13 is constitutional. We will show the court that Proposition 13 is sound policy benefiting all California property owners. By basing property taxes on the ability to pay at the time of voluntary purchase, and guaranteeing certainty as to what taxes will be in the future, Proposition 13 protects taxpayers from losing their homes to the tax collector. These benefits are available equally to all property owners."

But, also, I had to admit this was the ultimate test for Proposition 13. "There's no appeal from the U.S. Supreme Court, so this is life or death for Proposition 13."

Joining me at the press conference that day was attorney Jay Curtis, who HJTA had hired to help co-ordinate its effort with Los Angeles County's attorneys to defend Proposition 13. Nordlinger had filed her suit against the Los Angeles County assessor.

Yes, this was the same Jay Curtis who debated Howard Jarvis on Proposition 36. Curtis would be one of many attorneys working on behalf of Proposition 13. Besides

Curtis and the L. A. County attorneys, HJTA's own General Counsel Trevor Grimm and newly hired Director of Legal Affairs Jon Coupal were thrown into the breach. Eventually, the County decided to add the services of former United States Solicitor General Rex Lee, then president of Brigham Young University, to argue the case before the court. One of Lee's law partners at the Sidley and Austin firm was former California Governor George Deukmejian, who also participated in the case's preparation.

"Off with Its Head!"

The lawsuits challenging Proposition 13's constitutionality set off a flurry of activity. Major private studies were completed on how to restructure the property tax system if Proposition 13 were no longer the law. The media speculated about possible court decisions and radio talk show hosts alternatively tried to soothe listeners' fears or whip up anger over the fate of Prop 13. The legislature and governor got into the act with a study and a bill.

The bill by Assemblyman Johan Klehs declared that Proposition 13's acquisition value property tax scheme would remain in effect for two years even if the court found it unconstitutional, so that the legislature could produce an alternate system. The governor signed the bill. Separately, the Senate produced a two-year study which ended up recommending a split-roll property tax system if Proposition 13 were overturned. The proposal found few supporters.

On the public relations front, a war was being waged over whether Proposition 13 was indeed fair. In one television debate with a member of the Nordlinger legal brain trust, I discovered that they had looked up my home purchase record with the county to make a point that I was defending the Proposition 13 formula because I was a long-time homeowner reaping big benefits. I could see the disappointment in my opponent's eyes when he admitted that I bought my house the same year Nordlinger did and was paying higher taxes than my neighbors.

The special Senate Commission on Property Tax Equity and Revenue that was studying alternatives to Proposition 13 invited HJTA to testify. We gave them more than they bargained for. Through its foundation, the Howard Jarvis organization hired a number of well-known political economists and asked them to take a crack at preparing an alternative to Proposition 13, requiring only that they create a system that would protect homeowners who relied on Proposition13, that would achieve equality in the eyes of the law, and that would be as revenue neutral as possible. Making arrangements with the commission's chief consultant, Jonathan Lewis, we brought all the professors and economists to one meeting and allowed them to make their presentations. The session went on for over four hours.

Professor Alvin Rabushka from the Hoover Institution at Stanford called Proposition 13 "superb." He thought it worked well but, if tossed out, he recommended rolling back all property taxes to the 1975 level and requiring surcharges on other taxes to make up the difference.

Pepperdine University's Gary Galles recommended that property be reassessed at its current market value with a mandatory cut in the tax rate to achieve equity but said that in this plan, as in all plans, someone would be hurt.

Rodney Smith and Craig Stubblebine of Claremont McKenna College offered a system to cap spending by local governments to protect taxpayers. Responding to tough questions, Stubblebine told commission members, "You're arguing that the people should accept a lower standard of living so that government can have a higher one. The people complaining about not spending enough are from the public sector. I don't hear the private sector screaming."

The most provocative suggestion came from economist Arthur Laffer. He began by saying that Proposition 13 had been a tremendous benefit for the state, spurring massive economic growth. His suggestion to deal with the property tax program if Proposition 13 were eliminated: do away with the property tax altogether, substituting a flat income tax and a value-added business tax.

HJTA considered all its options but had not settled on a replacement plan by the time the Supreme Court hearing took place in February 1992. The *San Francisco Chronicle* of February 19 said, "Some analysts think the most likely result of a court decision invalidating California's property tax system ... would be a quick and successful tax-cutting initiative ... The issue will be dominated by the Howard Jarvis Taxpayers Association ..."

I predicted that if Proposition 13 were overturned, Governor Wilson would be forced to call a special election in 1993 to allow the people to vote on an alternative.

The battle was about to be joined in the Court.

The *Long Beach Press-Telegram* knew how it wanted the Proposition 13 case to turn out. On the morning of the Court hearing, February 25, the paper's editorial cried, "Off with its head!"

Before the U.S. Supreme Court

The key to determining Proposition 13's constitutionality was answering the question: "Was the system created by the initiative rational?" Were all people protected in some way so that the law did not discriminate against any class of taxpayers? This rationality argument would be the crux of the oral arguments.

Trevor Grimm and I settled into the courtroom seats along with defendant Kenneth Hahn, the Los Angeles

County assessor, and no relation to the long-time Los Angeles County supervisor with the same name. Grimm hoped to take notes on the proceedings so we could be prepared for the battery of reporters setting up their microphones outside, but a court guard told him to put his pen away. Only attorneys sitting at the counsel table and reporters in their proper area could write while the court conducted business. Well, it's said that the pen is mightier than the sword but we had been disarmed!

The one-hour oral argument opened with Stephanie Nordlinger's attorney Carlyle Hall arguing, "There's nothing to justify why one group ... should pay higher amounts than the favored group." Because Nordlinger paid higher taxes than neighbors with comparable homes who just had owned their homes longer, Hall said Proposition 13 was "irrational."

Justices Antonin Scalia and Sandra Day O'Connor appeared skeptical. "It seemed to have solved the problem that people can't keep up with (taxes on) unrealized gains in their homes," Scalia said, then drew a laugh as he summed up his position: "It may be rough and ready, it's not perfect, but it's close enough for government work."

Staying on the key point of a rational tax system, Justice O'Connor asked, "Do you think that the California scheme can rationally be related to the problem of people on fixed incomes being taxed out of their homes?"

Hall responded that the tax system was irrational because it was not related to ability to pay and that it benefited the rich. He tried to defend his charge by comparing his client's taxes to a mansion in Beverly Hills, but Justice David Souter interrupted him.

"I didn't ask you about Beverly Hills mansions," he said, "I asked you for the kind of person in the middle ... we're trying to find a standard taxpayer here, at least a peg to judge rationality."

The charge that Proposition 13 favored the rich would

be buried by a study released that year by the University of California, paid for by the state government. "The Future of Proposition 13 in California" by professors Arthur O'Sullivan, Terri Sexton, and Steve Sheffrin found that if the Proposition 13 property tax system were replaced on a revenue-neutral basis by the system operating in California before Prop 13, low income taxpayers would pay more and high income taxpayers would pay less.

Hall urged the justices to view Proposition 13 in light of the West Virginia ruling they made, overturning the similar tax system as violating the equal protection clause of the United States Constitution.

Rex Lee defended Proposition 13. "The only question is whether California's acquisition system furthers some legitimate state purpose and it clearly does," he told the court, referring to people keeping their homes.

However, Justice John Paul Stevens commented that "there's something counter-intuitive" about a system where people pay much more than neighbors to receive the same police and fire protection. Stevens also countered the argument that inflation was driving people from their homes by offering a suggestion. "There's another solution for some of these elderly people who have suddenly found their $10,000 homes are worth a million dollars. Some of them can sell those homes and still live, you know."

True, and some did. But those comfortable in their homes did not want to be forced to move by potential high taxes or the lure of big profits. Even if they sold their homes, buying a comparable home would eat up the money they received in the sale. And, the percentage of million-dollar homeowners was tiny.

It always is unwise to predict the outcome of a case based on the questions from judges. Nonetheless, Jon Coupal and Jay Curtis, sitting in the attorney section of the court, both were counting the number of justices who were asking increasingly tough questions of Nordlinger's attorney, and, who seemed to be indicating that they were not convinced that Proposition 13 violated the equal protection clause of the constitution. When that number reached five justices, Coupal and Curtis looked at each other and smiled. They would have stood up and "high-fived" each other had that not been a serious breach of courtroom decorum.

Immediately following the hearing, we walked down the magnificent, wide marble steps in front of the Supreme Court building to meet the media. There was a forest of microphones, many cameras, and print reporters. They all crowded around on this cold day, along with a number of California lawmakers and congress members who had listened to the arguments. We all gave our opinions of the hearing—mine were "cautious optimism"—but who really knew?

One of the camera crews in the crowd was ours. We had hired a crew, and as Stu Mollrich, who had put the plan together, described it, "We did a video news release, pre-edited footage which we put up on satellite for the stations to grab and use in evening newscasts" throughout California.

We knew the interest in the court case back in California and also knew that a number of stations, particularly the independents, would have little access to pictures of the event. We would accommodate them by sending back pictures, but of course, we were sending back what we wanted the viewers to see and hear. The clips were used by a number of California television stations.

Every Headline in the State

On June 18, 1992, the United States Supreme Court ruled Proposition 13 was constitutional by an 8 to 1 vote. The lone dissent came from Justice John Paul Stevens.

Stevens wrote, "It would obviously be unconstitutional to provide one (neighbor) with more or better fire or police protection than the other; it is just as plainly unconstitutional to require one to pay five times as much in property taxes as the other for the same government services."

The problem with Stevens' argument is that property taxes never were a fee for service. In fact, under the ad valorem system of taxation that existed before Proposition 13, and which still exists in many states, some people in more valuable homes do pay five times as much in property taxes for similar government service.

Justice Harry Blackmun delivered the majority opinion. He wrote that Proposition 13 did not discriminate. "Newer and older owners alike benefit in both the short and long run from the protection of a 1% tax rate ceiling and no more than a 2% increase in assessment value per year."

Additionally, the majority found, "The appropriate standard of review is whether the difference in treatment between newer and older owners rationally furthers a legitimate state interest."

Blackmun went on to say the Court found two good reasons to uphold Proposition 13.

> We have no difficulty in ascertaining at least two rational or reasonable considerations of difference or policy that justify denying petitioner the benefits of her neighbor's lower assessments.
>
> First, the state has a legitimate interest in local neighborhood preservation, continuity, and stability ... The state therefore legitimately can decide to structure its tax system to discourage rapid turnover in homes and businesses, for example, in order to discourage displacement of lower income families by the forces of gentrification, or of established mom-and-pop operations by newer chain operations.

> Second, the state legitimately can conclude that a new owner at the time of acquiring his property does not have the same reliance interest warranting protection against higher taxes as does an existing owner already saddled with his purchase, does not have the option of deciding not to buy his home if taxes become prohibitively high. To meet his tax obligations, he might be forced to sell his home or to divert his income away from the purchase of food, clothing and other necessities.

Much of this "rationality" argument had been made in one form or another over the years in defense of Proposition 13. In fact, before the vote on Prop 13, Neil Jacoby, one of the preeminent economists supporting the initiative, said in a speech at the UCLA Business Forecast Conference on March 16, 1978: "Stability of home or apartment occupancy is an import social goal. The present tax system weakens our society by threatening to force people out of their homes."

Fourteen years later, the United States Supreme Court said the same thing.

By chance, two days after the court decision, President George H. W. Bush was scheduled to speak to a special Saturday morning meeting of the Howard Jarvis Taxpayers Association in Universal City.

Twelve-hundred people strong came out to see the President and to celebrate the Supreme Court victory. In my opening statement, I grabbed a stack of different newspapers from around the state in each hand and held them up to the audience.

"Every headline in the state," I said to a cheering audience and smiling president. "We won! Prop 13 is constitutional!"

PART EIGHT

Fighting Back:
Proposition 218

Cracks in the Dam

If Proposition 13 was like a dam built against the ever-rising tide of taxes, it soon suffered from cracks. The Howard Jarvis Taxpayers Association often was like the little Dutch boy sticking fingers into holes in the dike. The cracks around Proposition 13 began soon after the election. New fees and charges were imposed; there were old, narrow revenue-raising devices, particularly the creation of assessment districts, which were adapted for broader, general governmental purposes.

HJTA was able to plug some of the holes. We stopped the plan to charge an "excise tax" for the privilege of using property. We also plugged an attempt by local governments to declare that pension plans actually were voter-approved indebtedness and that property taxes could be increased to cover increased pension costs. A bill by Assembly members Mike Roos and Ross Johnson signed by Governor Deukmejian limited that practice.

The fight often occurred on the local level, such as the time Santa Cruz County decided to create a county service area to fund police by levying a specific fee against property. The fee was as high as $2500 a year. Taxpayer activists Lee Phelps and Carolyn Busenhart led a local taxpayer revolt gathering thousands of signatures and forcing the authorities to rescind the tax.

However, government kept coming with creative strategies to raise revenue. It poked so many holes in the dike, that even though we tried to plug them all, the water, or should it be said the tax dollars, kept on flowing out of taxpayers' pockets into government coffers. While Proposition 13 established important tax limitations on government, as Howard Jarvis predicted, many bureaucrats, full-time anti-13 employees, stayed up late at night trying to figure out how to get around them.

Courts helped the bureaucrats along. The *Farrell* case allowed general taxes without votes of the people to stand until the decision was undone by Proposition 62, but then, even this measure kicked around the courts for years. During that time, it was ignored by charter cities, the larger cities in California, and in some cases, the law was ignored even after the California Supreme Court ruled Proposition 62 constitutional nine years after it passed.

The *Sinclair Paint* case opened the doors for additional fees. Sinclair Paint Company sued over a law that added a fee to a can of paint that was supposed to pay for damage done to people poisoned by lead paint. The Sinclair Company claimed it never used lead paint but the court approved the legislative bill, which attached the fee to all paint cans.

The court in the *Sinclair* case said that the word *tax* "has no fixed meaning and that the distinction between taxes and fees is frequently blurred taking on different meanings in different contexts."

The full force of the Sinclair decision is just starting to be felt as fees are being proposed for all sorts of products and businesses.

Much time was spent by HJTA in dealing with clever ploys to get more money from taxpayers. Legislation was sponsored and measures were put on the ballot by HJTA with little success until these end-run taxes, fees, and assessments got out of hand and started to sting. Then the people rallied around HJTA's Proposition 218 to give themselves the right to vote on many of these fees, assessments, service area charges, and revenue enhancements—whatever moniker the bureaucracy wanted to call them. We liked to call them what they really were—taxes.

As an attempted safeguard, Proposition 218 provided: "The provisions of this act shall be liberally construed to effect its purpose of limiting local government revenues and enhancing taxpayer consent."

But, before any taxpayer protection could work, it had to be passed by the voters.

"Limited Only by the Limits of Human Imagination"

Proposition 13 came into being to protect property taxpayers, but property taxes were again on the rise. Now, however, they were being called assessments, charges against property that were listed as line items on the property tax bill. Just look at all the charges added to your property tax bill below the line separating land and improvement values from the rest of the items on the bill. To the property taxpayer, it did not matter what the taxes were called. It just got them boiling mad, much as tax increases had done for the country's founders. Consider the opening of my op-ed piece in the August 15, 1991 *Los Angeles Times*:

> The "mob" opposing a school maintenance assessment district in Orange County was described as "almost maniacal" by Jerry Sullivan, a trustee of the Huntington Beach Union High School District.
>
> The "mob" that raged against Britain's infamous Stamp Act in Boston was described of "ill humors" by Francis Bernard, royal governor of the Massachusetts Bay Colony.

> There are great similarities between the spontaneous outburst of California property owners to the imposition of taxes in the form of assessment districts in the summer of 1991 and the colonists' reaction to the British Stamp Act of 1765.
>
> Members of the Sons of Liberty tarred and feathered stamp agents to protest the tax, which required that stamps be affixed to such things as business licenses, legal documents, diplomas and newspapers. Modern-day tar and feathering of officials who voted for a new tax on property comes in the form of recall petitions.

This Orange County tax revolt over a school assessment district was one of many examples of taxpayers continuing the Proposition 13 tax revolt when local governments, with assistance from the courts, found a way around Proposition 13's property tax protections.

The assessment district approach to tax increases was made-to-order for government. The move to go to these property tax assessments grew slowly at first after Proposition 13. However, they had become enough of a threat that HJTA sponsored a bill in the legislature in 1987 to require a vote on assessments. Over the course of nine years, HJTA sponsored seven bills to get a handle on the problem. After one defeat in front of a legislative committee, the chairman acknowledged that there was a growing problem with these non-voted property tax assessments and urged taxpayer groups and local governments to get together and work it out. But representatives of local governments were not interested in working anything out because assessment districts were becoming cherished revenue sources for them and they did not want citizens to interfere with their plans by getting a vote on revenue-raising proposals.

True assessment districts are set up to pay for capital improvements that will have a direct benefit to neighboring properties. The benefit can be calculated and each property receiving the benefit is obliged to pay its proportionate share. True assessment districts have a long history going back to ancient Roman roads and English sea walls. But many of the California assessment districts that sprang up after Proposition 13 passed were bogus. A number of assessment districts were based on the California Lighting and Landscaping Act. This act can be found in the California Streets and Highway Codes. You would think when these assessments were used, they would have something to do with streets and highways as was originally intended. But assessment dollars were used for parks, community colleges and football stadiums; anything for which officials could drum up a connection between property and some supposed property benefit.

In many cases, the benefit connection was pretty thin to the point of being transparent. One of the most outrageous assessment district proposals was floated in the Ventura County seaside town of Port Hueneme. It amounted to a "view tax." The better you saw the ocean the more you paid.

The assessment was actually to maintain beach parks. However, in the city's report on the assessment, it suggested that those living closer to the ocean, especially those with a view, got the most benefit. This assessment thereafter was tagged the "View Tax."

And, there were no discounts for foggy days.

More than half of the Port Hueneme property owners affected by the assessment filed a written protest, normally enough to kill any assessment. However, the City Council was able to overturn the protest by mustering a four-fifths vote of the council, a little-known provision found in the law at the time that meant when you played poker with the government on any assessment district, government started the game holding four aces.

Whimsically, I wondered in a *Los Angeles Times* article: "If assessments are appropriate for ocean views, why not assessments for certain city views? Doubters should remember that beauty is in the eye of the beholder who sets the rates."

Accompanying the article was a picture of downtown Los Angeles shrouded in smog with the caption: "Is this view worth taxing?"

Despite having the upper hand legally, the Port Hueneme City Council withdrew the "View Tax" under withering political and editorial pressure.

What really got governments salivating over assessment districts was a 1992 California Supreme Court decision called *Knox vs. City of Orland*. Orland is a city in Glenn County about 90 miles north of Sacramento. Using the Landscaping and Lighting Act, the City drew up a district essentially to maintain its parks. A flat fee was charged on every living unit within 27 miles of the park so, if an apartment had 20 units, each one was assessed a fee. Under traditional benefit assessment theory, the closer you were to the lights and landscaping, the more you benefited. However, basically, this Supreme Court decision said that if you lived 27 miles away, your property got equal benefit of a landscaped and lighted park as did the property across the street from the park. Furthermore, the court allowed this assessment to pay for maintenance of an existing facility, opening the door for mischief on a wide scale.

The court's reasoning would establish the assessment district as every government's favorite revenue-raising device. Benefit assessments had been stretched like Pinocchio's nose, beyond their original size and intent.

They now were virtual property taxes, with no limits and no vote of the people—just like before Proposition 13 passed. As attorney Brian Curry, who followed these things, said after the ruling by the court, "Assessment districts are now limited only by the limits of human imagination."

Imagine how that made taxpayers feel. If allowed to go unchecked, Proposition 13, essentially, was dead.

More and more assessments found their way on to property tax bills, so many that one northern California county had to redesign its tax bill. In the City of Los Angeles, there was talk of a benefit assessment to fund the police department after the people had voted down a direct police tax measure.

With the growing tide of assessments threatening to wipe out Proposition 13's property tax protection, and after a number of failed attempts to get relief from the legislature, the Howard Jarvis Taxpayers Association qualified a measure for the ballot to give the voters some power over assessments.

Proposition 218 would bring some balance to the decision-making process about assessments and strengthen taxpayer protections in a number of ways. It would change the way assessments were affirmed. Prior to Proposition 218, if a property owner did not send in a protest, his or her property was essentially counted as a "Yes" vote for an assessment.

Under Prop 218, every property owner would receive a mailed notice to return, voting "Yes" or "No." A majority of "Yes" votes were needed to approve assessments. The vote would be proportional, so if one property received a larger benefit than another and, therefore, had to pay a larger amount, that property's vote would be weighted accordingly and counted more. This plan was adopted from long-standing assessment law.

Proposition 218 also would require a vote on property-related fees and require that those fees not exceed the cost of service provided. The initiative also would settle a long-standing dispute and order charter cities to put any proposed general tax increases before the voters for a majority vote. Perhaps overlooked at the time, the initiative also made it easier for citizens to propose tax-cutting initiatives on the local level by lessening the number of signatures needed to get them on the ballot.

Long-time columnist and *Sacramento Bee* Editor, Peter
Schrag, scoffed at the proportional voting on assessments
in Prop 218. He wrote in his book, *Paradise Lost*: " . . . in
true Hamiltonian fashion, (Proposition 218) gave electoral
privileges to the rich and wellborn—and excluded those
not so blessed—in a manner that had not been seriously
proposed in America since the abolition of the poll tax."

Jon Coupal, who crafted the measure then as HJTA's
director of legal affairs, responded: "Prop 218 did not
change the law in this respect. Assessments in all states,
including California, apportioned the amount of the
assessment based on the benefits to the individual parcels.
This only makes sense. If one needs a 50-foot pipe to hook
up to a sewer, why should the homeowner have to pay the
same as someone who needs a 200-foot pipe? When it
comes to a strictly property-related service, fairness dictates
that those benefited more, pay more. We cannot fathom
why liberals such as Schrag cannot understand this simple
concept."

The idea that all parcel owners, not necessarily registered
voters, had the right to vote their approval or disapproval
of benefit assessment proposals, was seized upon by
opponents to attack Proposition 218.

You wouldn't want Saddam Hussein to vote on an
assessment in your neighborhood, would you? He could,
if he had the controlling interest in property here in
California that was going to be assessed. That was the
message. Truly. Besides, had Hussein owned property in
California *prior* to Proposition 218, he still would have had
the equal power with other property owners to protest any
proposed assessment.

The California League of Cities, taking a much more
aggressive political stance than at any time in its history,
led the campaign against the initiative. The league claimed
it was not using taxpayer dollars that filtered through city
fees to the organization to run the campaign.

The biggest problem for the "NO" campaign was that the voters could see what was going on. Property owners could see the ever-growing list of assessments on their tax bills and they knew they did not vote on many of them. They thought that Proposition 13 had taken care of this problem.

But once again, government's greed led to its undoing. A few months before Proposition 218 was on the ballot, the Los Angeles Community College District decided to levy a landscaping and lighting assessment on over one million properties throughout the huge community college district. The district wanted $12 for each property to fund the assessment. How did the district officials arrive at the figure? They took a poll. The district polled people in the area and determined that at $12, the people would not complain.

Among the improvements planned under the assessment that was supposed to go for landscaping and lighting was the construction of a $2 million football stadium scoreboard at one school, and a $6 million equestrian center at another.

With a straight face, a majority of the Community College Board members had to say that this equestrian center, maybe 20 miles away from assessed property, somehow benefited the property. And the amazing thing is—they said it!

Or, at least, they tried to. A hue and cry rang out throughout Los Angeles over this assessment plan. The district held public hearings and confronted rooms full of angry residents. The district registered a total of 30,000 written protests. However, under assessment protest provisions, this total hardly was enough. Protesters needed 500,000 protests to be successful, an impossible number to get in a short time. But the protests and negative stories in the media were enough for the board to reconsider its decision. It put the measure on the ballot for voter approval, where it was defeated easily.

Meanwhile, the clumsy handling of this assessment district served as kindling for Proposition 218's victory fire.

Prop 218 Victory

While the Proposition 218 campaign never received the attention that the Proposition 13 campaign did, nevertheless, it was hard fought. Opponents of Proposition 218 relied heavily on professional political consultants. The HJTA campaign was led by HJTA's Executive Director Kris Vosburgh, Proposition 218's drafter, HJTA attorney Jon Coupal and me.

On election day, I did a last-minute television broadcast on Bill Rosendahl's cable show, amazingly, the only television program dealing exclusively with state and local political issues left in Los Angeles. Then I was finished with the campaign. Walking from the studio, I checked phone messages and returned a call to Tom Hiltachk, an attorney who had worked with us on the Proposition 218 effort. He told me he decided that since it was election day, he could visit with some friends who had worked on the "NO" campaign. They told him that their polling showed Proposition 218 was going to lose by 15 percentage points and that they had called their clients already to tell them they had at least a 10-point win. Tom wanted me to know what he had heard. We had no money to poll so I had no idea how the election would turn out.

Reporters were given telephone numbers to reach either Jon Coupal or me after the polls closed. Coupal called me right after 8 P.M. and said a reporter called him and claimed that exit polls showed Proposition 218 winning. I said, "You're kidding," three times. Because of the information received from Hiltachk, neither Jon nor I were prepared to believe it. However, as the positive results continued to come in, Jon and I had to completely shift our planned media comments from explaining defeat to cheering victory.

Proposition 218 carried the state with more than 56% of the vote. That is the last time I will listen to polls, especially when they come from the other side, even if it is election day.

Dave Doerr wrote of Proposition 218's victory: "A nearly 20-year effort to give voters the right to vote on local tax increases came to an end in 1996 when voters approved Proposition 218 . . . The Jarvis organization was the primary driving force in the campaign . . ."

Senator Tom McClintock said, "Proposition 218 simply restored the central tenet of Proposition 13 and that is, governments have to live within their means and if governments want to raise taxes, they have to ask permission of the taxpayers."

While gloom and doom projections were made after the election about irresponsible voters not raising taxes, voters took their responsibilities seriously. Some taxes were defeated, but others passed. Lakewood Mayor Bob Wagner told the *Los Angeles Times* after his citizens passed a tax increase: "Residents have shown they are willing to listen if public officials can make a good case for a tax, but it is not something I want to do very often."

Raising taxes is not something the voters want to consider often, either.

So, the battle ended and the people had the right to vote on taxes by whatever name they were called. This time the clamps were on good.

Maybe.

Dan Wall, then working for the California State Association of Counties, said sometime after the election, "There were a number of clever people who devised Proposition 218. But there are an equal number of clever people who are going to try and interpret it."

PART NINE

A Never-ending Battle

The Attacks Continue

In early 1999, I was in Sacramento to attend a meeting of a state commission to which I was appointed. I had retired as president of HJTA and Jon Coupal was now president. When I checked my phone for messages, I listened to one from Dane Waters who ran the Initiative and Referendum Institute in Washington, D.C., asking me to speak on Proposition 13 at a conference he was putting together. He specifically wanted me to defend Proposition 13 because another speaker, Peter Schrag, was on the program. Schrag's new book *Paradise Lost* had attacked Proposition 13 and Waters wanted a balanced program. I turned off the phone and looked up at the guy who was waiting to head off with me for dinner and said, "Peter, they want me to beat up on you at the initiative conference."

Schrag's attack on Proposition 13 and, more specifically, the initiative process in general, was not unexpected. Reading Schrag's book, one finds his solutions for solving the problems which he believes are caused by Proposition 13. The numerous reforms he applauds fall into two categories: one is tax increases, the other is making it easier to raise taxes. His is a "New Deal" approach to problem-solving that we can dub the "Old Deal" now.

Conspicuously absent from Schrag's list are any reforms that would deliver government services more efficiently and economically, although he acknowledges that Proposition 13 accomplished some of that. The Prop 13 reforms are the kinds of changes in which voters are interested. The idea of solving problems by raising taxes does not sell so easily today.

Government efficiency and reform is possible. David Osborne and Ted Gaebler pointed out a number of examples of positive government reform in their book, *Reinventing Government*. They cited the city of Visalia, which responded to Proposition 13 by pioneering creative programs that cut costs, resulting, a few years later, in a budget surplus almost as large as the city's operating budget.

Schrag is an idealist. He once said he would prefer that government be run using a civic textbook rather than the constitution. Idealists are important. We must measure ourselves against the "ideal" from time to time to see how we are doing. However, when it comes to the political world, as with the legal world, Oliver Wendall Holmes hit the mark when he said, "The life of the law has not been logic, it has been experience."

It was experience that compelled taxpayer revolutionaries to put tough limits on government's taxing power while putting themselves, the taxpayers, into the tax decision-making process with a right to vote on taxes.

Still, those who want to see things run in a different way, either because they want more money for their special interest or, like Schrag, believe that there is a better way for government to work, continue pressing for changes in Proposition 13.

Schrag saw government paradise in Pat Brown's administration, which was an unparalleled period of public building, from universities to roads to waterworks. As an example of this paradise found, in the first paragraph of his book, Schrag praises the nearly "free" higher education system that once was offered in California.

Yet, he doesn't bother asking, free to whom? Indeed, Schrag later acknowledges that "the state's taxpayers had been asked to shell out so generously" for the state's higher education system which allows tenured professors to teach only a couple of classes a week, yet provides them with healthy retirement benefits.

More importantly, never once does Schrag note that the Pat Brown building boom occurred at a time when taxes were lower as a percent of personal income than they are today. Priorities have changed since Pat Brown's day, with a much larger portion of the government dollar now going to health and welfare services and government employee wages and benefits.

While admitting the tax revolt was the result of an out-of-control property tax system, Schrag nevertheless sought to discover some hidden malignant meaning in Proposition 13. He divined that a sense of community had been lost because taxpayers (meaning here, whites) became selfish with a desire to deny public services to minorities.

This theory has been debunked by the landslide support for the Los Angeles school bonds, as well as passage of other big city school bond proposals. While Los Angeles school children are overwhelmingly minority, huge majorities have passed school bonds across every segment of the ethnic rainbow.

There is no race card when it comes to taxes. Culturally and historically, no matter race, creed, color, or religion, all people are in agreement on taxation. They're agin' it!

At the time of Proposition 13's 20th anniversary, the *Los Angeles Times* sent out a reporter to write an article from the angle that Proposition 13 was a conspiracy against minorities. The article never appeared. When I saw the reporter months later and asked him why not, he said, "We didn't find any bad guys." No conspirators, no conspiracy.

Proposition 13 has been accused of all kinds of perversity over the years. I think that some of the accusations are worth repeating, only because they are so absurd they raise doubts about the validity of all claims made against Proposition 13. Be prepared. Some of these charges border on hysteria.

Already mentioned earlier in this book were the serious, unsubstantiated and frankly foolish charges that Proposition

13: (a) helped free O. J. Simpson, (b) allowed Polly Klass's murderer to escape a police dragnet, and (c) caused the collapse of Bay Area freeways after the Loma Prieta earthquake.

How about Prop 13 being a contributing factor to the riots that followed the original police verdicts in the Rodney King beating case?

Or how about an editorial in the 1990 *Bakersfield Californian* that asked the question: Could it be that Proposition 13 is killing children because Kern County did not have enough measles serum? The answer the editorial gave was probably not—but the question was asked nonetheless.

Proposition 13 was linked to hate crimes by syndicated columnist Tom Elias, and a *San Jose Mercury News* writer called it the "great rapist" of the state's educational system.

A California State University, Sacramento, physical education professor told the *Sacramento Bee* that the slide in children's fitness toward obesity began with Proposition 13 because towels for showering after physical education classes were no longer given out to students so they skipped the classes.

Proposition 13 was responsible for the Orange County bankruptcy because, some have charged, lower revenues forced county financial officers to gamble reserves in risky investments.

On the lighter side of Proposition 13's devilishness, a *Pasadena Star News* music writer blamed Proposition 13, along with the decline in mainline church attendance, for the shrinking pool of choral singers. I can't be sure but it probably has to do with music education in the schools.

Finally, in a list that can go on and on, a high school track and field coach blamed Proposition 13 for his team losing shot puts. Five seconds to figure this one out yourself—because of Prop 13, the coach maintained that the grass around the track was not cut as often as it should be and the shot puts were lost in the tall grass.

Despite the constant barrage against it, on the whole, voters seem quite comfortable with Proposition 13. Yet, the law is not written in stone. A simple majority vote of the people can repeal or amend Proposition 13. If the measure were as evil as some portray, the people of California would have done away with it long ago.

Like Grandmother's Quilt

Money magazine's cover story of the January 1994 issue was titled "The Tax Revolt that Wrecked California." Authored by journalist and writer Richard Reeves, the long piece carried familiar anti-Prop 13 arguments but opened with the outrageous accusation that Proposition 13 may be culpable in the murder of 12-year-old Polly Klass. Reeves argued that if the Petaluma police department had been able to afford advanced communication equipment, they may have been able to rescue the girl before the killing.

The New York–based magazine was surprised at the response the article received. Many letters came from Californians differing with Reeves' opinion about Proposition 13. The readers' response gave the editors of *Money* an idea to set up a California conference on Proposition 13. It was arranged to be an all-day affair with heavyweights like CNN's Lou Dobbs and *L. A. Times* editor-in-chief Shelby Coffey set to speak. The opening event was a debate between Reeves and me. The magazine publicized the conference, especially to its California readers. It was held on the UCLA campus—and hardly anybody came.

The auditorium was practically empty. Probably half those in attendance were scheduled speakers during the course of the day. Not a surprise, really, when you consider the conference was held on a weekday when most *Money* magazine readers were working, and at the end of the school year when UCLA students were dealing with final exams. The truth is, most Californians already had made up their minds about Proposition 13 years before.

Money editors should not have been surprised about the reaction of their readers to tax-cutting Proposition 13. The idea of saving money is what the magazine is all about. I wonder if the editors recognized the irony of that January cover with the main story splashed across the page: "The Tax Revolt that Wrecked California," and the smaller slash across the corner of the cover promoting another story inside to its readers: "How to Cut Taxes 30% State-Federal-Property."

Accepting the debate with Reeves was not HJTA's only response to the one-sided article. We appealed to the editor's sense of fairness to balance the article with a column of our own or at least a staff-written correction to some of Reeves' charges, but our request was denied. We submitted a letter to the editor with no result. So, we decided to buy a full-page ad in *Money* to present our story. Not a bad racquet for *Money*. They print a one-sided article, deny an opportunity to respond, and then get paid big bucks to publish a response.

Our ad was published in June and was buried in the back of the magazine. It expressed outrage over the charges made against Proposition 13 and cited positives about the measure, including referring to a recent letter written by an elderly couple expressing their gratitude that "they could live in the house they love for the rest of their days."

In the ad, we asked those who attacked Proposition 13 to answer a few questions:

> How is it that property taxes under Proposition
> 13 have been the most reliable revenue source,
> growing almost 10 percent a year for over a decade?

How is it that California had a state budget of about $52 billion in 1992, more than three times larger than the $15 billion budget of 1978, out stripping both inflation and population growth?

If Proposition 13 caused the deficit in California's budget this fiscal year, a decade and a half after it passed, is it then responsible for the tax surplus of six years ago when a billion dollars was returned to taxpayers?

Most of the charges that Reeves made in his article and repeated in the debate had been leveled at Proposition 13 by others.

There was the question of property tax equity or fairness under Proposition 13. Critics have been quite blunt. Assemblyman Tom Hannigan said, "There is nothing fair about it (13), nothing equitable about it." The equity question was raised mostly about similar homes standing side by side but paying different taxes depending on when they were purchased. The U.S. Supreme Court dealt with the constitutionality of this issue by saying Proposition 13's formula was reasonable. In truth, property taxes were rarely equitable under the old ad valorem tax system. A dozen years before Proposition 13 passed, the Assembly Revenue and Taxation Committee reported equalization of assessments was "more myth than a reality."

More expensive homes pay more in property taxes but do not get extra police protection or get more fire trucks sent to put out a blaze than less expensive homes. A fee-for-service scheme has never been the nature of any property tax system.

Howard Jarvis said what really was unfair was the system prior to Proposition 13, that when a new neighbor bought the house next door, all of a sudden, your property taxes were based on what your neighbor wanted to pay for a house. Said Jarvis, "What we did cured 99 and 99/

100% of this thieving system they had before. There's no way in God's green world that you can have a perfect system as long as you have a property tax at all .... The whole property tax system is tied to market value. Under 13, the guy that pays $80,000 for the house makes his own market value. He controls his own decision, he decides what the price of his house is going to be, and he decides what his taxes are going to be."

As Karen Nolan of the *Vacaville Reporter* commented, Proposition 13 was like her grandmother's quilt: each patch was different, but stitched together, it kept everybody warm. Under Proposition 13, each property may have a different tax amount, but every one in the community is protected.

The fairness question is often raised in the context of the tax cuts somehow hurting the poor. Lawyers from a Bay Area legal foundation once filed a lawsuit to "liberate" Alameda County from Proposition 13 because they contended the tax restrictions limited the amount of money available for health care. Robert Kuttner titled his book on Proposition 13, *The Revolt of the Haves*. However, defending people in their homes was important. The University of California study already mentioned, which showed that the acquisition value system was more geared to ability to pay than the ad valorem tax system, answered the fairness question.

Reeves complained that the state and local governments were taking in fewer taxes than before Proposition 13. The old saying that there are lies, damned lies, and statistics was invented for government number crunching. The numbers Reeves' used concerned taxes but ignored a bevy of new and increased fees and assessments. Pepperdine economist Gary Galles attacked the Reeves' figures used in the *Money* article saying that the premise that Prop 13 "decimated government funding" was false. He called Reeves figures "highly misleading ... because it measures the wrong thing."

It is not my intent to get into an economic discussion here, however, at this point in time, most agree that all levels of government are collecting and spending more money in constant dollars than they did prior to Prop 13. Then, why don't we get the quality of services we used to get? The answer is the money goes for bigger government and the expansion of government employees' wages and benefits, the largest portion of any government budget. The money is not related, necessarily, to better service.

Reeves saved his most savage criticism for education funding under Proposition 13. He wrote: "Prop 13 at its meanest and most enduring was generational warfare. The old chose themselves over the young in 1978 . . . they voted to trade lower property taxes for themselves in exchange for diminished education spending for other people's children—many of them, it happens, black and Hispanic kids."

Let's get one thing clear. The state spends much more per pupil in constant dollars than before Proposition 13 despite the fact that California has many more pupils because of its population explosion over the last 25 years. Each of these students—all students of all ethnicity and races—receive the benefit of more money spent on their education than California students did in the 1970s. How that money is spent is worth examining.

During the debate with Reeves, I quoted an Anna Quindlen column from the *New York Times*: "In our town, the school system is spending just over $12,000 a pupil. That should make it roughly the elementary equivalent of Stanford. Instead, people who are able to, sent their children to private and parochial schools because they believe the public schools are substandard. This makes us like many other urban residents in the country. The cupboard is bare, and taxpayers everywhere are looking around to see where the money has gone. And, the answer, in so many cases, is that it has been badly spent."

While California dropped in school spending relative to some other states since Proposition 13 passed, it was not because California was spending less per pupil. Part of the education funding problem is that the state dictates how the money is spent in many instances. Given the *Serrano* decisions requiring "equal" spending per student, it would be difficult to return the obligation of major funding for education to the local level. The state should be the collector of tax dollars for the schools but, like a retailer with the sales tax, it should just act as a collection agency. Retailers take in sales taxes and ship them to the government. Likewise, the state should take in tax revenue then send it to local school authorities as block grants with no strings attached. Let the education decisions be made on the local level.

Another argument goes that Proposition 13 forced local governments to chase after "big box" retailers, large retail outlets that produce fat sales tax revenue for local government. The argument is that property taxes alone from residential, commercial and industrial property do not cover the costs of government service because the property tax is capped. Noted land use planner and critic William Fulton said that this policy of seeking "big box" retailers leads to "sales tax canyons ... simply to empty passing wallets." The state intensified the problem when it moved property taxes from local governments to the schools to solve state-funding problems in the early '90s recession.

Many cities before Proposition 13 survived on sales taxes alone; there were 30 that levied no property tax at all. Still, a new formula for sharing the sales and property taxes between state and local governments could help relieve any pressure on local governments to make planning decisions. It would take a simple change of the law, not a change in Proposition 13.

Proposition 13 said that property taxes should be "apportioned according to law." Many charge that the wording gave the state power over the property taxes while reducing the taxing power of local governments.

Not so fast. The California Supreme Court considered the loss-of-home-rule argument in the *Amador* case and found the "petitioners' fears in this connection seem illusory and ill-founded."

The Court said the Legislature already had control over property taxes and pointed out some examples in the constitution such as granting property tax exemptions. The Legislature used Proposition 13 as an excuse to get more involved with local revenues.

As to losing taxing power, certainly local government cannot raise property taxes on a whim anymore. However, as tax expert Dave Doerr pointed out, following Proposition 13, local governments have added plenty of taxing powers that they did not have prior to 1978. Parcel taxes came into existence after Proposition 13. Counties and specified cities were given flexibility to impose additional sales taxes with voter approval and the tax-raising authority of charter cities was extended to general law cities and counties. Utility taxes and business taxes can now be enacted with appropriate voter approval.

Perhaps the most controversial sections of Proposition 13 were the provisions that taxes raised by the legislature and local special taxes voted on by the people required a two-thirds vote. These provisions have been attacked constantly by opponents as being undemocratic. The cry is that one "No" vote should not have the weight of two "Yes" votes.

On the other hand, Milton Friedman told the *Copley News Service* during the 1978 campaign that the two-thirds vote might be the most important feature of Proposition 13, to prevent other tax increases from making up for the property tax cut.

Howard Jarvis defended the two-thirds vote for taxes in an editorial rebuttal on Los Angeles's CBS television affiliate by asking:

> Is it unfair that the legislature needs a two-thirds vote to override a governor's veto? Nationally, is it unfair that Congress needs a two-thirds vote to override a presidential veto? Or that a two-thirds vote is needed to kill a filibuster? Is it unfair that the United States Senate must get a two-thirds vote to approve a treaty; or impeach a president? Is it also unfair to require a two-thirds vote to propose a constitutional amendment in Congress; then get a two-thirds vote in three fourths of the state legislatures to approve the amendment?
>
> How about California courts? Is it unfair that we require a two-thirds vote for a decision in appellate court cases; a three-fourths vote in civil cases; and a 100 percent vote in criminal cases?
>
> The two-thirds vote is a protection written into the U.S. Constitution. It protects our freedom for quick fixes, irrational thinking, and over-zealous legislators.

There is no more important power of government than the power to levy taxes. The two-thirds vote is a protection against a tyranny of a majority to take property ... that is taxes ... from the people. It is right and proper that we make it difficult to do.

We must be wary of the warning from eighteenth-century Scottish historian Alexander Tytler: "A democracy cannot exist as a permanent form of government. It can only exist until a majority of voters discover that they can vote themselves largess out of the public treasury." Tytler's warning specifically was that "the majority always votes for the candidates promising the most benefits from the public treasury."

Interestingly, Richard Reeves expressed similar concerns in his book, *American Journey*, in which he retraced the steps of Alexis De Tocqueville around America. "When employees of government—teachers in the public schools were a good

example—provided significant campaign funding and
volunteer campaign workers to help elect legislators, they
were essentially trying to hire their own bosses, the men
and women who regulate their numbers, salaries, benefits,
and working conditions."

However, there is a persistent war against the two-thirds
vote. After a number of attempts, an initiative was passed
in 2000, lowering the two-thirds vote requirement for
passing school construction bonds to 55%. The two-thirds
vote requirement for bonds was not part of Proposition 13;
it had been in the state constitution since 1879. It took a
$30-million dollar campaign to pass this proposition.
However, with the success of this measure, legislators and
bureaucrats started talking about lowering the two-thirds
requirement to raise other taxes.

Finally, there is the whispered attack that taxpayers don't
know what they're doing when they put a tax-cutting
measure on the ballot. It's often stated that they are not
sophisticated enough to write tax law. That issue popped
up as soon as Proposition 13 passed. On Howard Jarvis's
Meet the Press appearance in 1978, the final question to
him came from Neal Pierce of the *National Journal*: "Doesn't
it really boil down to, that you have put a proposition on
the books, and you really don't know what its effects are
going to be?"

Jarvis answered, "Well, that is what happened when
they wrote the Constitution of the United States. Nobody
knew what it was going to be. We know one thing it (13) is
going to do: It is going to cut taxes in California, and that is
the objective."

I have my own response to the criticism that taxpayers
don't know what they're doing when they advocate for
tax change. This country was founded on a tax revolt when
American colonists dressed up like Indians and threw tea
into Boston Harbor to protest a tax on tea. When the United
States became a country, the first tax revolt was the Whiskey
Rebellion. Let me point out that no taxpayer threw a barrel

of whiskey overboard anywhere to protest the tax on whiskey. That's because we taxpayers know what we're doing!

"Thank Goodness for Proposition 13"

Proposition 13 must have done something right to command so much support and respect over the years. Of course, it made property taxes more reasonable and kept people from losing their homes to the tax authorities. But, also, it did something revolutionary when it came to taxes. For the first time, certainty about taxes belonged to the taxpayer instead of the tax collector.

An acquisition property tax policy makes taxes predictable and removes the problem of subjective assessments by assessors, while protecting homeowners against prohibitive property tax increases. Taxpayers knew that their property taxes would be 1% of the market value, in most cases the purchase price, and, in the future, would go up no more than 2% a year.

Adam Smith stated in his *Wealth of Nations*: "The certainty of what each individual ought to pay is, in taxation, a matter of so great importance, that a very considerable degree of inequality ... is not near so great an evil as a very small degree of uncertainty."

Proposition 13 had captured Smith's notion of certainty.

For government, the system works, too. Property taxes in California were increasing about 10% a year statewide before the '90s recession and continued to produce positive revenue growth despite the recession. Normally, under the market value system, when property values drop during a recession, taxes must be reduced. Because, under

Proposition 13, many properties are paying taxes on assessed values below even the recession-reduced market values, taxes on these properties do not have to be lowered. In fact, they still can be raised 2% if inflation increases that much or more. The government does not suffer a severe shock to its revenue collection. During the 1990s recession, one Los Angeles County Assessor's Office official acknowledged that advantage and told the *L.A. Daily News*: "Thank goodness for Proposition 13."

The same thing was being repeated in the difficult budget days of 2002 and beyond. A December 10, 2002 *Los Angeles Times* article said that while tax revenue on income, capital gains, sales and other revenue sources are down, property taxes are an increasing revenue source for government. As California officials wrestle with a budget deficit of more than $21 billion, taxes on real estate, according to Ventura County Assessor Dan Goodwin, are "keeping it from being a disaster."

Of course, the taxpayers benefit, too. During recession, when taxpayers have fewer dollars coming in, politicians can no longer look to the property taxpayer as easy prey and jack up the property taxes.

As Proposition 13 neared its 25th anniversary, reports of dramatic property tax increases in New York City and a number of states were making news. But in California, the protection that Proposition 13 brought to homeowners when it first passed 25 years before was still working its magic.

Imagine what would have happened to the poor property taxpayers in the Silicon Valley during the roaring late 1990s. Refurbished garages were selling for a million dollars. When some rich, high-tech entrepreneur came in and bought the garage, made into a home for that kind of money, under the old property tax system, all the neighboring homes would zoom up to a stupendous new market value and many a long-time homeowner would be forced to sell.

Even Proposition 13 critic Lenny Goldberg, of the public employee union—supported California Tax Reform Association, had come to the conclusion, "If we didn't have homeowners property tax protection (with Proposition 13), we would need it now."

How much money Proposition 13 actually saved California property taxpayers is a hard question to answer. Dave Doerr made a calculation in his book, *California's Tax Machine,* on the 20th anniversary of Proposition 13, and concluded that taxpayers' relief amounted at a minimum of $100 billion to perhaps as high as $250 billion depending on how growth rate in property taxes and the property tax rate were calculated.

Of course, government thinks of these reduced taxes as lost revenue. Government officials talk about revenue expenditures as if tax cuts are a budget item. Part of the difference of opinion between government insiders and the ordinary guy on the street is that they speak different languages. Take the basic tax cut. For the average citizen, the money we earn is ours until we give it up to government in taxes. If there's a tax cut, then we get to keep more of our money and don't have to give it up. Government doesn't see it that way. In calculating the budget, a tax cut is considered a "tax expenditure," money that government could have had but does not, as if that money belonged to government which generously handed it back to taxpayers.

Here's an example from a couple of years ago on how the legislature proposed to cut the car tax. Normally, the legislature votes for a tax cut, the governor okays it, tax formulas are adjusted, your tax bill reflects the lower levy and you pay the smaller tax. Not this time. Under the plan, the legislature voted to reduce the car tax, the governor approved, but the tax rates were not changed. It was decided that the car tax invoice sent to taxpayers would reflect the full amount of the taxes owed on their cars under the current tax structure. Only after taxpayers paid the full tax—and a few months went by—would they receive a rebate check for the amount of the tax cut.

Governor Gray Davis explained his support for this plan by saying, "People don't appreciate the fact that they're getting a rebate unless they see it in their hands."

No doubt the rebate check would come with a self-congratulatory letter from the governor and legislators explaining how they were able to wrestle these dollars from the $13-billion state surplus.

This scheme, designed to show how fiscally prudent our government was, cost a whopping $44 million of taxpayers' money.

The $44-million figure covered the cost of mailing checks and processing paperwork over the two-year life of this scheme. Not coincidentally, the time lag brought us to the 2002 election. The $44-million cost did not include the loss of interest to taxpayers and the gain of interest money to the state because the treasurer would hold on to the money that should never have been taken from the people in the first place. But that's what happens when the politicians think it is their money.

What was the motivation of the original plan? Self-promotion for elected officials, pure and simple. In returning some of the surplus to the people who created it, politicians wanted credit and gratitude. The plan finally collapsed under public outrage.

It is not the politicians' money. That point was made long ago when John Randolph, a Virginia congressman in the early 1800s told his colleagues, "You enjoy the most delicious of all privileges, spending other people's money."

Still, spending taxpayer money is about the most important thing for many legislators. But I have learned it may not be the most important. I participated on a panel about the initiative process before a group of elected officials from around the country at UC Berkeley's Institute for Governmental Studies. I expected the usual hostile reception as I defended Proposition 13 and tax cuts. However, I was pretty much ignored by the legislators. Also on the panel was Mike Ford, one of the leaders of the Term Limit initiative that recently had passed in California. Ford was the target of the legislators' animus. I guess the only thing that angers some politicians more than having less money to spend is having less time in which to spend it.

"Maybe the Tax Rebels Had Been Right"

Twenty-five years after Proposition 13 passed, Nobel Prize-winning economist Milton Friedman looked back and said, "The political effect (of Proposition 13) was very good in moving us in the direction of lowering taxes."

Surprisingly, Friedman does not have the same animosity toward the property tax that many have. He felt the amount of property tax would be reflected in the housing cost and the cost would be adjusted according to the amount of property tax that had to be paid on the property. Yet, the average taxpayer has long been concerned with the property tax burden. As Dave Doerr pointed out, "The epochal changes in California's tax structure since 1850 all stem from an effort to provide property tax relief."

Even Peter Schrag begrudgingly acknowledged that while taxpayers could control sales taxes by controlling their spending habits, and income taxes depended on their income, "Property taxes were beyond the taxpayer's control. Twenty years later, some of their former opponents began reluctantly to acknowledge that on that point, maybe, the tax rebels had been right."

Others who sharply criticized Proposition 13 have

softened their tones. I recently participated in a political forum at the University of Southern California where former state Senator David Roberti said he appreciated Proposition 13 more now than when he was in the legislature, although he pointedly added he was not endorsing it.

Perhaps even more amazing, the *Los Angeles Times* started off its May 25, 1998 editorial on the 20th anniversary of Proposition 13 this way:

> Proposition 13 is 20 years old and it's time to proclaim the tax-cutting measure a stunning success. The ballot brainchild of Howard Jarvis and others has been vilified by critics for two decades and blamed for much of what ails California. But, at the heart of it, the measure did exactly what Jarvis promised. More important, it fulfilled the demands of California homeowners, many of whom legitimately feared that runaway property taxes would force them from their homes.
>
> Proposition 13 provided a substantial and permanent reduction in soaring property tax levels and brought stability to a tax system that had been rife with corruption and subject to the volatile whims of the housing market. Today the property tax formula of Proposition 13 is an integral element of California life.

Of course, the editorial went on to point out what it perceived as negatives with Proposition 13, but we'll take what we can get, and given the history of the *Times'* perspective on Prop 13, that is a lot.

If any critic of Proposition 13 wants to change it, the formula is simple enough. It takes a majority vote of the people. Yet, no one has really made an effort to change Proposition 13 significantly over the past 25 years because the people understand the measure stands as a shield between them and a sometimes too-greedy government.

In his recent study of the California electorate, which he discussed in his book, *A California State of Mind*, Mark Baldassre of the Public Policy Institute of California found that voters still have a powerful distrust for government that developed strongly at the time of Proposition 13. He felt this distrust prevented government officials from having the power they need over taxes to make life better in the Golden State.

But distrust in government is as old as this nation itself and was the reason for adding the Bill of Rights to the United States Constitution. Proposition 13 is in fine company.

PART TEN

The Legend Continues

Spirit of Prop 13

Proposition 13 lived up to that 1960s slogan: Power to the People. The *Los Angeles Times* understood this fact even two decades after the measure passed: "After the revolutionary Proposition 13 lanced state government, voters have consolidated power into their own hands and are clamping a tight hold on the purse strings. They mean to keep it that way."

Proposition 13 made two changes in giving voters more power. The voters have certainty in property taxes, and they have a right to vote on tax increases. It's a good bet both protections will stay in place.

Proposition 13 is a law like any other law. It has been amended over the years. Other alterations may occur. But the spirit of Proposition 13 will remain. Howard Jarvis recognized that: "Proposition 13 proved, beyond any reasonable doubt, that the people can achieve the kind of government structure they want if they are willing to fight for it. In an important sense, this realization is more significant than the actual victory of 13."

Thomas Jefferson wrote, "The good sense of the people will always be found to be the best army. They may be led astray for a moment but will soon correct themselves." Those of us who have faith in the people to control their own lives believe in Jefferson's words. That's why we are not afraid when special interests hoping to undo Proposition 13 start rattling sabers. The people know what's good for them.

Legend

If Proposition 13 had not passed, the world would look quite different. Would Ronald Reagan have been elected? Would the economic engine of the United States been unleashed to move toward freer markets and a freer world? Would the Berlin Wall have come down?

Well, maybe this is too much to put on the shoulders of a California property tax revolt, but who knows? Most everyone accepts the analysis cited by *Business Week* on July 17, 1978 that California had "staged the most significant tax revolt of modern times." That revolt meant that freedom was on the march.

In accepting the Thomas Jefferson Award for 1978, Howard Jarvis said, "About 15 years ago, a few neighbors in California met and decided long-entrenched political power had become unlimited, that the basic American principle, government must be limited, was being undermined, which power, if not curbed, made unlimited taxation and loss of individual liberty in America a certainty. We had two choices. To fight for liberty or give up. We decided to fight, not just for our generation but for generations of Americans to come."

Many legends have begun with the determination of ordinary people to fight for freedom.

Taxes have long been seen as something both necessary and as something to be feared. There is little doubt that fighting for freedom from taxes strikes a familiar chord in most people. It may be part of our inner make-up. The oldest writings, yet discovered, talk about taxes. From the fertile plain of the Tigris and Euphrates rivers comes a clay tablet, which warns, "You can have a Lord, you can have a King, but the man to fear is the tax collector."

The warning expressed on that ancient clay tablet can

be heard still in our modern culture. In the film *Samson and Delilah*, the tablet's sentiment is expressed almost exactly by George Sanders as the villian in the film: "I think one tax collector is worth a thousand soldiers."

The *Star Wars* epic, a myth created in our time, reveals in *Episode I* something in common with legends and stories told by other generations. The tale is propelled forward, as one character says, by the "tragedy of taxation."

And, who can forget George Harrison's plaintive call with the Beatles' song, *The Taxman*: "Should five percent appear too small, be thankful I don't take it all"?

Resisting taxes is in our blood. Yet, the tax revolt in California has been called radical. Dressing up as American Indians and tossing tea into Boston Harbor was radical. Lady Godiva's ride, a protest against high taxes, was radical. Proposition 13 was a tax revolt, but one carried out within the rules of the state constitution and it was not radical. However, followers of Proposition 13 were just as defiant and just as resolute as other heroic tax fighters.

Worldwide and nationally, there have been other tax revolts. Why is Proposition 13 special? Perhaps because of the characters, the larger-than-life fireball, Howard Jarvis, and the youthful, ambitious and thoughtful Governor Jerry Brown, among others. Perhaps because of the size and scope of the tax cut in one of the largest economies in the world. Perhaps because this tax revolt clearly changed the course of history and changed long-held attitudes toward government. Most likely, it was a combination of all these things.

But, because ordinary people joined together to take back control of their lives on a grand scale and to secure for themselves greater freedom, Proposition 13 has gone beyond its tax-cutting role. It has been draped in the robes of legend.

Index

A

Adams, James Ring 45, 54, 93, 99
AirCal Magazine 31
Alameda County 35, 107, 216
Allen, Howard 61
Amador case 106, 107, 108, 111, 183, 219
American Economic Association 85
American Tax Reduction Movement 141, 163
Anderson, Martin 129, 133
Anger, Ann 42
Apartment Association of Greater Los Angeles 73, 74, 85
Arizona Morning News 30
Assembly Democratic Caucus 98
Assembly Revenue and Taxation Committee 49, 66, 83, 107, 215

B

Bakersfield Californian 212
Baldassre, Mark 228
Bayh, Birch 137
Behr, Peter 83, 84
Bellows, Jim 76
Berkeley Gazette 70
Betz, Chuck 42, 54
Bird, Rose 109, 111
Blackmun, Harry 190
Boston Globe 37, 100
Boston Tea Party 13, 20, 23, 25
Bradbury, Ray 163
Braude, Marvin 100
Brennan, William 180
Brezhnev, Leonid 101
Briem, Ray 51
Brown, Dennis 98
Brown, Jerry 31, 51, 62, 82, 84, 103, 104, 105, 106, 136, 142, 233
Brown, Pat 82, 83, 127, 128, 129, 210, 211
Brown, Willie 66, 70, 157
Busch, Ed 30
Busenhart, Carolyn 195
Bush, George H. W. 167, 191
Bush, George W. 140